Just

Something Special

By

Jay Kay

Dedicated to

Wendolyn

"I will always love
you Wendy"

I

Working a new assignment in Kansas City, I report to work at the Kansas City Royal Hotel. Right across the street from the Royals Stadium, it was a recent purchase from a company called HBE, later to be the Adam's Mark hotel chain. I am hired on as a Restaurant Manager, hired to supervise a renovation. The hotel has two restaurants; one is a coffee shop and the other is a fine dining restaurant. The new concept was, you order a cut of steak, tell the chef how many ounces you want, the chef will then cut it to order and we will prepare it for you. This was a new concept back then. It was about 1980. The hotel has two bars. One of the bars is on the lobby level and the other is on the rooftop. The rooftop lounge has live entertainment and a spectacular view of the city. I experienced the world's longest interview with this company when I joined them. I left Hartford Connecticut in the morning, changed planes and had breakfast in Pittsburgh, Pennsylvania. I then flew to St Louis where the home office was located and had three interviews with four different vice presidents. I had lunch in St. Louis and then flew to Kansas City that night.

My interview there was to take place the following morning. I was on Carte Blanche and was told to enjoy myself until the end of the weekend. I inquired with the travel secretary what the end of the weekend was and she told me I was flying back to Hartford Sunday night. It was a long weekend but I took the job. That is where I met Wendy. She was a young, very attractive and great humored cocktail waitress with a smile that would make anyone melt.

I used to hang out there as it was also my job to babysit that operation on the Lounge Manager's days off. I didn't really mind as the scenery was always pleasing to the eyes, if you know what I mean. Wendy and I never dated during my employment there, as it was against company policy. I did occasionally walk her to her car for security reasons. I did however live with a lobby bar bartender while I worked there. It was very discreet and I was never much for following rules.

After eight boring months of supervising a renovation that never started, I decide it's time to leave. The company bought nine hotels and tried to renovate them all at the same time. I just got tired of waiting. I am not very happy with work or my personal life. The lobby bartender and I have broken up and she has moved to Florida. Prior to taking this position with this company I applied to a larger hotel corporation, as I had a friend who recently went there as a Vice President. Things were just taking too long. I made some calls and took a few interview trips. One trip was to New York and one to New Jersey, at different times. After negotiating and making some hard decisions, I take a position with this larger hotel company. I am slated to move to New Jersey in two weeks. A farewell party is planned in my honor by my friend and executive chef, Peter. It's to be held at our apartment complex. It was a cool complex as some of the Kansas City Chiefs lived there. Constant parties can only describe my life in that complex at the young age of 25.

The party was nice as Peter prepared several outstanding hors d'oeurves, including Shrimp Cocktail and a lot of other upscale hor's d'oeurves as he was a class chef. There was lots of liquor and 8mm porn films running constantly. Showing porn films with both sexes in the room always helped to get the juices flowing. Someone usually got laid afterwards. It's a great party and it is growing late as I have to drive to New York in the morning non-stop. Midnight comes and I make the smart decision to walk home. No driving involved so it's a no brainer. I lived one hundred feet away.

A knock at the door 30 minutes later, yields two coffee shop waitresses who wanted to come in for a night cap or maybe something else. There is this thing about women I have learned over the years. Women love to screw guys who are leaving town. No one will ever know or talk, it is a good philosophy. This was starting to look like a threesome. These girls were sisters, (exciting in itself) but only average looking, however I was super tired. I decline as I am a little drunk and packed and ready to go to New York in a few hours. My plan was to leave at 6:00am.

I get ready for bed and an hour later the phone rings. It's the gate. It's a great community as you cannot gain access through the gate unless the resident allows security to buzz you in. It has save my ass several times when I had a guest and one wanted to see me. This guy was cool because if you told him you weren't home, he told your visitor you weren't home. He never let on that he actually talked to you. He was very cool and very discreet. I actually used to bring this guy little gifts from time to time to show my appreciation. Working in the hotel industry, you run across little trinkets, like promotional stuff, key chains, t-shirts, tote bags and stuff like that. He always appreciated the gesture. I ask who is at the gate, and he replies, Wendy. I think for a while as Wendy and I have never dated and it's the only Wendy that I know. Now I am back to my theory about "guys leaving town". I tell the gate to let her in out of pure curiosity.

Wendy was five foot three, one hundred ten pounds, brown curly hair, beautiful brown eyes and very shapely. She was a very attractive woman. Her smile would light up any room. I let her in and she skipped the small talk and we went right to it. The next few hours was consumed by awesome sex. I think my theory about men leaving town is now pretty solid. It's now four in the morning and Wendy is departing. But I feel, after the last two hours that **_something special_** has just happened. She leaves as I grab a few hours sleep or try to and depart for New York City in the morning.

I pack the rest of my things; I thought, and embark on the 15 hour drive to Stamford, Connecticut, which was my training property. Adrenaline drove most of the way as I was on a cloud nine of sorts. I had the entire trip to remember last night and how she made me feel. It was comfortable, secure and the sex was awesome. Arriving at nine at night, I checked into the hotel so I can report to work in the morning with my new boss. Upon awakening and showering, I realized I had left my dress shirts and dress shoes in my closet in Kansas City. I guess my mind was on something or someone else. I bolted to the local men's store to take care of my deficiencies and return promptly for my meeting. All goes well as I am given the day off due to scheduling conflicts that had given my trainer the day off. It was a busy weekend at the hotel and most people took Monday off to get some well needed rest. This was great, as I was still in Lala Land thinking about Wendy.

2

Work was pretty standard but I couldn't stop thinking about Wendy and that "***something special***". It was a feeling that I don't think I have ever felt before. Wendy and I talked several times per week and after a short few weeks I realized I didn't want to live without her. I weighed my options before asking her to move out here as the hotel business has you relocating every eighteen months or so. Settling down was nowhere in sight most of the time. This type of life is not for everyone especially if you want to settle down and have a family. I already had an ex-wife and a son and I was in a new zip code. I asked her anyways to pick-up and move to New Jersey. This would happen after I arrived at my home property, got an apartment and got settled. Her answer didn't come immediately and I asked her not to rush her decision as a young girl moving half way across the country is a big move. I wasn't very hopeful, after all our past consisted of just the one night. Her answer came a week or so later and it was yes. I immediately became very nervous as I wasn't sure what the hell I was doing. I convinced myself, this is what I wanted.

Life in a new job in the hospitality industry is tough, as the hours and days are long. You try to get familiar with everyone and everything as quickly as possible. I was living in the hotel as part of my contract for 30 days to allow me to find a suitable apartment. I was mostly consumed by my work. Wendy and I spoke very frequently, perhaps nightly after I got off work.

I think I fell in love with her over the phone. We talked about everything as it was like dating but over the phone. I think this is where we established our great ability to communicate. There were no facial expressions or leaving the room and slamming the door. We were on the phone. As time went on, I became excited with anticipation of her arrival, with only now a hint of doubt.

I found an apartment, leased it, and awaited the arrival of my stuff from the big moving truck. It was estimated to arrive in seven to ten days. I was still busy with work as one day the phone call came that my stuff will be there in the morning. They gave me only a two hour window to supervise the unloading of my stuff. It was a second floor apartment and I didn't care, as I didn't have to lug that furniture up the stairs (no elevator). Of course I wasn't thinking, what happens when I move out? Hmm! Two hours was an amazing window in which to unload an apartment full of stuff, but it got done. I quickly sign the paperwork and returned to work. I just figured I would unpack my stuff later.

I guess we don't realize how much stuff we have until we move. Each night after work I unpacked boxes, boxes and more boxes. It took about a week to get settled in. It was tough after working a twelve hour day to come home and unpack for two to three hours, for the next seven days. I was excited about Wendy's arrival so I didn't care. In the middle of unpacking and getting to the end of this tedious task, I realized I had no kitchen stuff. Hmmm! If you have been a Chef like me and have been the hospitality industry for a while, you collect some really cool stuff. I am missing all my pots, pans, skillets, knives, and all of my other cool stuff. This sucks as now, I have to file a claim with the moving company to find out where my missing stuff is. I am assuming that the movers saw my cool kitchen stuff (as they packed it) and decided to relocate it, but not in my direction. The moves with this hotel chain was very efficient as all you had to do was relocate your ass and they did EVERYTHING else, pack, ship, etc.

To make a long story shorter than it has to be, Peter, Chef Peter kept my cool stuff, as the moving company confirmed that it was never loaded on the truck. I left Peter in charge of my move on the Kansas City end. It was a poor choice I guess. I replace all my cool stuff with the essentials, not so cool stuff, to make my apartment fully functional. Now I am ready to accept Wendy, who will eventually become the love of my entire life.

The phone calls continued on a daily basis. This was actually a good thing as we continued learning about each other. I have always believed in communication is the key to most successful things and the lack of it is the key to most failed things. There was a lot of learning going on and we grew closer keeping in mind, at this point we only had the one night and several hours of phone calls. The phone calls eventually evolved into phone sex on occasion. Being apart with only fantastic memories of the one night we had, created a great deal of horny anxieties. She was reluctant at first and thought that this was dirty and inappropriate, but she soon came around and began to look forward to it.

Now the ball was in her court to get there. Everything was on target and no one was changing their minds. So now it was a matter of setting dates and just doing it. Wendy gave her notice, said her good-byes, packed her car and was on her way. As a hint of doubt lingered, I became more excited about her arrival. Finally she arrived. Wow! I was now the happiest man in the world. My attitude was so positive I couldn't stand myself and the company thought I was simply amazing. Things at work were really turning around in my favor. All my efforts became fruitful. Everything I did came out smelling like roses. A positive attitude in life is crucial to everything that happens in your life. Believe me. I gave her a hug that lasted what seemed like days and a kiss that would make your spine tingle. I loved the way she made me feel.

Now is the time to do all the painful stuff for Wendy, like finding a job, car registration, title, etc, etc. It doesn't take Wendy but a few days to land a job. She gets a job at local cocktail lounge called Mando's. That was her current profession and she was good at it. This was perfect. Starting the next day, she is excited and I am excited for her. Being only twenty years old I am a little concerned as cocktail waitresses are sometimes put in situations that can be potentially dangerous. The goal in this industry is to make great tips. Sometimes you need to make a member of the opposite sex think that you are interested in them. With hope in the eyes of the bar patron, your tips are bigger. You just have to hope you don't run across a nut job waiting for you in the parking lot or some fatal attraction freak follows you home. It's a thin line. Most of the bars I worked in always had a safety policy of walking the girls to their cars every night without exception. So I wasn't going to worry, too much.

3

This bar was a fricking gold mind. I wished I owned it. Opened from 11:00am until 4:00am, it was the second home for many. It had a lunch crowd at the noon hour, a happy hour crowd, and an evening crowd, as well as the late night crowd. It had Juke Box entertainment, great drinks and of course a great staff. The entire staff made great money as it was always busy. Wendy worked the night or late night shift and I never had a problem with that. It was also the local hang out for my staff after work, seven nights per week. I held confidential management meetings there in the afternoon, which was a good reason the leave work early. Hey, when you go to work at six am, your eight hours are up after two in the afternoon. I remember a bartender named Dominic who worked the day shift and appeared to always be trashed. We would ask him for change for cigarettes and give him a ten dollar bill and he would give us change for a twenty. Not believing this was possible; my assistant would repeat the request, give him a ten and get change from a twenty. We always gave it back to him in the tip as I knew his drawer would be twenty dollars short. She loved it there as she always had a great love for money. I didn't ask her to pay any bills. All the money she earned she could do with as she pleased. I made a really good salary so I paid all the bills. She bought food, paid for dinner out once in a while and basically had no financial worries. I wanted her to be happy and she was. She paid her own car insurance and her car was paid for. I would estimate that she made forty thousand dollars a year (1980), good money!

She worked there for over two years and flourished the entire time. I never interfered with her work as I would visit her regularly. There was always a hotel group there, sometimes large, sometimes small and sometimes just me. I never got jealous about the way she made money. She was a professional and a very friendly person from birth. Remember I was a bartender and I know how to make money. I do however, remember that sometimes as the hotel staff gathered, drank and departed, the bill was sometimes an issue. If you drink $9 worth of liquor and leave me $10 to pay the bill, there becomes a problem as sometimes there were over a dozen of us. A $12 tip on a $100 bill doesn't cut it. It was always one bill and always cash. You guys didn't leave me enough to properly tip the waitress. Everyone knew she was my girl. Several times I had to kick in the difference as I was usually the last one to leave. I never told Wendy but, I sure let the short changers know about it the next day. It was a job security thing for them. I have written a book on tipping, so let's not get me started.

There were some issues however, that developed from working there. The first issue was Wendy's age. She was 20 years old and old enough to serve liquor but not old enough to drink. Back then it was very customary to have a "shift drink" or two after work. I worked 10 plus hours a day and most days even more. By the time I finished a long day at work and a long night of

drinking I was usually sound asleep
after 4 am when she came home.
The drinking after work didn't really
bother me as she was never
hammered when she got home. My
problem was the integrity of the
bartenders serving a minor. I know
about the hush, hush, wink and a
nod. DUI's were no big deal back
then as there were no Dram Shop
laws. It started to bother me when
my second issue arrived on the
scene. Back in the 1980's cocaine
was widely used in powder form
everywhere, as it had really just
gained popularity. Giving it to my
girlfriend with that after work cocktail
was now concerning to me. Now she
would come home higher than the
Empire State Building and staying up
for hours on end. My precious sleep
time with her started to erode. This
developed into her purchasing
cocaine for recreational use at home
as well as a standard late night
Mando's thing. I was not a virgin to
this drug and I was okay with it for
quite some time. I enjoyed it as much
as she did and we began to enjoy it
together.

Wendy got a little bit too deep into this addiction enough that she had to get a SECOND job to support her desires. Additionally, there is a separate chapter in this book, which may be a result from this initial addition. You have no clue as to what happens to her later.

4

Life at home was great. She and I
were both young back then, so we
were very active. We were always
going out, never at home. On the
occasions we were home, I cooked
as it's something I have always loved
to do. As we both worked in public
places, wherever we went we both
knew several people. It was great to
be respected by the community and
to have so many friends. Our favorite
place was an establishment
ingeniously named "The Pub". It had
great food and a great staff. We used
to hang there together and
separately. Wendy always wanted to
go to Mandos on her time off and at
first I didn't realize why until later. It
was for the cocaine.

Sex at home was more than exciting.
She was a wild thing and I loved it. It
was never boring as new and
different things happened on a
regular basis. There was sex with
cocaine, sex with food, sex in all
kinds of positions and even mutual

masturbation resulting in great endings. There were bananas, cucumbers, strawberries, peanut butter, chocolate and whipped cream. I will let you use your imagination to render the appropriate uses for these items. It was a very horny time for both of us and unusual things happened all the time. Wendy had a collection of photographs of the men's penises when they were masturbating. Photos of rock hard dicks were an obsession with her for her entire life. Wendy always masturbated on her stomach, which I thought was strange. She said it was the only way she could get off. She was young and didn't know her body very well at that age. On several occasions, we would be watching TV and I became horny. I began stroking my unit and she would begin masturbating under her bathrobe. We would break out some cocaine and the whole event would end with Wendy on top and mutual simultaneous orgasms. Wow, I loved that.

There was also a neighbor who lived in the apartment behind us who worked out in the nude. Her shades were always open and her house faced an entire apartment complex. I'm sure she wanted to be viewed. I always thought that it was very sexy. It used to get me excited enough to make me have to release the pressure it created in my balls. I never did tell Wendy about that. She really didn't need to know. Now that Wendy was coming out of her shell, being away from home, she started to mature into a very sexy woman. Her dress code at work only specified wearing a Danskin and a skirt. This was pretty simple one would think. The only creativity Wendy could think of was what she wore underneath the skirt. She was starting to buy thigh-high stocking, garter belts and special panties. Get your mind out of the gutter folks; there were no T-backs back then, except in strip clubs. She said it helped her tips, and it certainly didn't hurt when she came home after a few shift drinks all horny and wanting to have sex. You can wake me up in the middle of the night for sex ANYTIME!

We also had the respected life we led. We attended benefit dinners, private parties, galas, and a lot of stuff going on in New York City. She loved the city and it was only 20 minutes away, so it was extremely convenient. She worked nights and I worked all the time in the beginning. We spent time together when we could and we tried to match our days off whenever possible. We would go out to dinner and clubbing whenever the opportunity presented itself. After I got settled in my job, which requires more time upfront and less time after a while, we would take trips. The beach was not very far away, as a three hour journey was not long, as if you lived in the New York City area that could just be a nasty day on your commute to work. Besides while Wendy was performing her normal fellatio on the trip, time seemed to fly. My parents had a beach house in Rhode Island and it became our favorite spot. My parents were hardly ever there and they didn't start renting the place out until years later. There was nothing but privacy, the ocean and us. That's all we needed. After a little trip to the beach house, the batteries were all recharged and we were ready to go back to work.

She wanted to buy a new car and of course I was there for her. I co-signed the loan, without reservation as she probably made more money than me. Servers, the good ones, make real good money. Included in this purchase, was teaching her to drive a stick shift. It's a lot like teaching a loved on how to play golf. VERY FRUSTRATING!!! I will not go into details of the training process, as if any of you have gone through the process of the previously mentioned tasks, you realized what a strain it is on any relationship.

I had a son from my first marriage that was four years old at the time. I would see him whenever time permitted. He lived in Connecticut with his Mom and she understood that I lived two hours away. I made reasonable efforts to take him for weekends and vacations whenever possible. Remarkably, Wendy took him under her wing, for me. She was a special woman, splitting my time with her, knowing I needed to spend time with my son. This included holidays, weekends and some of our vacations. Wendy spent time with him as if he was her own, never complaining ever, about splitting time with my son. Wendy had no children of her own at this time and she showed me how unselfish she could be. Again it was ***something special***.

5

Cocaine was a part of our lives. I never did it on a regular basis until Wendy started to do it. What a feeling. It was not an addiction for either of us at first. It was like sex. It's something you wanted to do whenever you could. It felt good and we both made plenty of money so there was no financial strain. We never missed a day of work and were very responsible with our financial obligations so we were not addicted like a junkie. Every year, my brother, a bean counter, had a party at the beach house the first weekend in June. It was the party of the year. There were three bedrooms at the beach house and a loft and lots of decking outside, so there was room to sleep usually 20 or more. Let's face it after drinking in the sun all day, eating clams, lobster, and chowder, who cared where you crashed. We never let on to anyone that we used cocaine. It's a family thing. Get it?

There were always a couple of Hobie Cats on property for anyone's use and the Atlantic Ocean provided more than enough excitement. The trick to using a Hobie Cat is knowing how to flip it and how to right it. You dump it during a lightning storm, to prevent from getting electrocuted, and then right it (upright) when it's over. We ended up on a deserted beach once after heading for shelter in front a huge thunderstorm. The island was only accessible by boat and there was no one there. It was very cool until we tried to leave. The other trick you need to know about sailing a Hobie Cat in the Atlantic is how to launch in heavy surf. Any person with catamaran experience knows that you count the waves. The seventh wave is always the biggest. The key is to find the biggest wave and launch during the smallest wave, the first. Once you break through the surf, you raise the main sail and off you go. However, if the smallest wave is over six feet, you are kind of screwed. After several attempts and unable to raise the main sail before the boat flipped, I decided I wasn't falling off ANYMORE! So I strapped myself in and away we went. Big

Mistake! The boat flipped anyway and now I am strapped to the boat under water. Oh shit, I'm going to die! Talk about thinking under pressure, this should be a movie. Not really excited about checking out in my mid twenties and watching my life flash before my eyes, I finally got out with a little lung water and pure exhaustion. After all that excitement it was time to take a break. We drank some beers (we never lost the beer) and smoked a half a pack of cigarettes. After an hour passed, the sea calmed down, we launched successfully and returned back to the beach house for a well deserved nap.

Hobie Cat people are *special* people, a little nuts. One year during the annual party, my brother decided to go for cocktails at a bar called "Bloody Mary's". There was one problem as this bar was 18 miles away, by boat. The bar was on Block Island, only accessible by boat and my genius brother took the Hobie Cat. Leaving at three in the afternoon, one would expect he would be home for dinner. It's about one hour out and one back, with one hour of drinking time. While he was gone, Wendy and I went to the local seafood market to get dinner which consisted of lobsters, clams, corn on the cob. I was making Clam Chowder, as I do every year, from some Cohogs we pulled out of the bay that day. While in the market I read a newspaper article on the wall about the sighting of a 16 foot Great White Shark off the coast where the house was. I remarked to Wendy that I thought the article was bullshit. The female clerk waiting on us now, commented that it was her husband, the fisherman for the store who spotted the shark and that it definitely was not bullshit. I became a little concerned as the shark sighting was two days prior and it was spotted in the same water my genius brother was in on the way to Bloody Mary's. My problem was that the shark was the same length as the boat he was on. This would be a mere snack for the shark. All worn out from the sun, sex, cocaine and alcohol, I dismissed any further concerns.

We return to the beach house and I started on the chowder. The rest of the preparations are made for dinner so we can just fire it when it was time. Potato Salad, Cole Slaw and a large tossed salad were made as well as corn on the cob and baked potatoes all to be cooked in the fire pit we had built. The Clams were covered in seaweed, the potatoes in foil and the corn in its original husk. The lobsters would be steamed in seaweed as well. Yummy! Now it is 4:00pm and time for a nap. Wendy and I retire for sixty minutes of just sleep. Five o'clock comes and it's time to prepare for one great gastronomical experience. There are people everywhere who we knew, as this was the third year I attended this event. A little cocaine to wake up followed by a Jack Daniels on the rocks and Wendy and I am good to go now.

I start the fire pit and all the cooking, a labor of love, which I never minded. The reward was too great. I love to eat. The remaining friends prepare the tables, dishes, lobster crackers, etc. New beer is iced and we are on target by 6pm. All the food is done to perfection and there is only one thing missing, my brother. I put this in the back of my mind as he is an avid sailor. He knows catamarans inside and out. I have no doubt about his boating skills. I forgot to mention he left Sandy, his girlfriend of a few years behind as she thought it was too dangerous to go on that particular journey. She was probably right.

We ate and I didn't feel the need to alarm anyone as we were young and fearless. Dinner is over and it's seven pm and no brother. Hmmm! Sandy is worried as I am also becoming concerned. The sun has set and it is dark. Wendy and I take a meeting in the master bedroom and I express my concerns. The master bedroom was the meeting place when you wanted privacy or you were in deep shit and needed a talking to. It was a special place. I love my brother and there is too much history in my family of people drowning, and the shark thing has now re-entered my mind. It's time to call the United States Coast Guard. I make the call; gave a description of the boat, his possible route and her sail numbers. Most people sailing catamarans don't file a float plan. I inform the rest of the guests as to my concerns and ask them not to worry as I was just taking, probably unnecessary precautions. Everyone is relaxing now as how could you not after a meal like that. Two hours has passed and the status quo has remained unchanged. I pick up the phone to call the Coast Guard for an update. There is no news.

As I hang up the phone, in walks my brother with the greeting "Hey, What's up?" perfectly healthy except for his BAC, which was probably pretty high, as was he. Again we take a meeting in the master bedroom and I express my concerns and he feels the love of a brother and his need to admit how stupid it was to be late. Remember there were no cell phones back then. I am sure we can all think back of some stupid things we did when we were young. By the way, leftovers at a clam bake are really not that good. It's like having sex with a condom.

The beach house was a great place, period. We went there for vacations, weekends and just day trips when my Dad was alive. We had dinner on the last night of a week's vacation there once. I remember it vividly as we were both out of cash, had about enough money for gas to get home and neither one of us was fond of credit cards. We went to a place called Georges, a great seafood restaurant. We agreed to charge the bill as we were leaving in the morning, back to reality, and cash would be available tomorrow. Dinner was great and it was just another fantastic week with my girl, Wendy. That **_something special_** just never went away. After getting the bill I presented my credit card for payment. No way Jose. They didn't take them. Between the two of us we didn't have enough cash to cover the check, not to mention the tip. Washing dishes was not an option. Hmmm! I asked the server what my options were and she said that they would take a check. I told her it was out of state and she said that was okay. I thought this was odd but it was acceptable to us as it was possibly the only way out.

This was in the 1980"s and a lot of restaurants didn't want to pay processing fees for credit card charges so they didn't take them. Boy, times have changed. We left the next morning and back to the grind.

6

Life is better in the Bahamas, they say and I'll tell you why. I had some time off coming and Wendy was going to get away for the weekend. I went to Daytona Beach to play tennis and hang out with an old and dear friend for four days. I was then going to drive to Miami to meet Wendy who was flying in from New York. I had a great time playing tennis with Gary. I used to kick his ass all the time when we lived up north. Now that he lives in Florida, he plays year round and I do not. The results were not pretty. He was my Room Service Manager before I joined this company. It was fun all the same. On day four I rented a car and drove four hours during Love Bug Season to Miami to pick Wendy up at the airport. We are going to spend the night in a hotel before taking a cruise to Grand Bahama Island. Love Bug Season is brutal. While making love all the time, these bugs expire on your windshield constantly. You wash the nose (of your car) daily and you go through washer fluid like drinking beer watching a football game. I went through a tank of windshield washer fluid in four hours.

When I finally got to the airport, it was great to see my baby as I missed her more than you can imagine. At this point we had not been apart since we first got together. We drove back to the hotel and she was bushed. She worked all night, packed and flew out early in the morning. I doubt she even slept. Throughout her entire life, sleep was never a priority with her. If something she thought was more important could be done, then sleep always waited or was omitted. We checked in to the hotel and unpacked as the best part of this trip was about to begin. While unpacking, Wendy shows me her surprise as she brought 2 grams of cocaine with her for the trip. Airport security as we all know, wasn't much back in the 1980's. I told her that it was not a smart move on her part, as I did not want to spend the rest of my life in a Bahamian prison. So we decided to get rid of it. We snorted all night long, as well as made love all night long. It was almost gone, but we saved a good bump for breakfast before boarding the cruise.

Packed and ready to go, we cleared security and I felt relieved. Complimentary cocktails were served prior to departure and Gin and Tonics were in high order. After four G/T's and a ¼ gram of cocaine up my nose, I am standing on the bow of the boat waiting for the crew to cast off. With little sleep, higher than the Empire State Building, the captain sounds the ships horn and I jump, no shit, 6 feet. We are under way. What a way to sail.

It's a five hour trip and I really don't remember most of it as Wendy told me we slept most of the way. We check into the hotel and unpack. As part of our package we receive $200 worth of chits to use at a local casino as well as two free drinks at a choice of local clubs. This is going to be a great weekend. We go to dinner and totally crash until the next morning. I think you know why, no sleep. I am up early and head for the pool. Wendy joins me a short while later and some guy named Dr. Alcohol presents himself at the pool for the morning workout. He is trying to get a tired, over traveled and lazy bunch, motivated to do a work out. There were three of us who decided to do this. I thought it would take away some of the partying pain. The first exercise was sit-ups. Dr. Alcohol counted them out, one, two, three, and that was it. A bottle of Champagne was then issued to everyone who participated, all three of us. Man this was going to be a long week. The work out session was now over. We hung out at the pool the first day and just slept. Finally regenerated, we were back to zero and got ready for dinner. Dinner was great and we decided to go for a walk on the beach. Wendy had a crazy side of her that I learned over the years. I am not sure if it was crazy or kinky, but her colors came true after dinner. We walked along the beach for a while and she asked me to sit down. I did, as I always trusted her. She was wearing a spaghetti strap top and a full black and white skirt that went half way down her calves. As I sat down on the beach she lowered me totally vertical and then mounted me. With no panties on she proceeded to screw my brains out on a public beach in front of several casual passerbyers. Wow, what a thrill and what an orgasm. It was all from the excitement of sex in public.

Gambling was also part of the package. They gave us a few chips to get us into the local casino and it worked. We had a few of their FuFu cocktails with hardly any liquor in them and gambled for two hours. We were Black Jack fans, both of us, and we did quite well. We walked away with $400 in our pockets and I didn't realize with Wendy's love of money, this became another addiction of hers later in life. She always did very, very well. The rest of the week progressed and it was relaxing not to have any deadlines or appointments or commitments. This was before the world was connected with the internet. There were no emails, no cell phones ringing, nothing but peace and quiet. If we wanted to take nap at three in the afternoon, no one was going to stop us. What a completely unwinding experience it was and we both needed it. We boarded the cruise ship that night to return and another five hour trip. This cruise was like a shuttle. Every day it sailed to Grand Bahama Island in the morning and back to Miami every night. It was totally different during the evening. The air was clean and the water was as clear as drinking water. There was a slight breeze with a temperature of eighty degrees. We took it easier on the way back than on the way there as we had no drugs for five days, but we were high on being together. Being with Wendy for me was like a child in a mother's womb. Nothing felt better.

We had some dinner and Wendy wanted to go to the casino. This is how the cruise line actually made money. Just not on Wendy. She always, over all the years, had the hottest hand for Black Jack. I accompanied her but did not play as my luck was not even close to her level. She did well as an audience collected as she approached winning two thousand dollars. It was simply amazing to watch her play. The cruise home seemed to take no time at all and soon it was time to disembark. We were spending the night in a hotel and flying back to the city in the morning. It was a great trip and one I will always remember. Getting home was a bit of a challenge as the travel agent messed up the tickets. We thought we were flying out at noon. The tickets were for midnight. I think we would remember that. The ticket agent who didn't belong in customer service, made it extremely difficult to get us back to the City. I summoned his supervisor, (usually works) and he got us home.

Most of our free time was spent at beaches. The Rhode Island beaches were our favorite. I grew up at Misquamicut Beach when I was younger and always gravitated back there. There were some great bars on that beach. There was rock and roll, and disco. That's all there was back then. These bars are lost dinosaurs as you could go in during in the day in you swim suit, no shoes, etc and listen to live music all day. We would jump in and out of the water; go back and forth to the beach and then the bar. There was Rock and Roll band during the day and during the darkness of night the bar turned into a discotheque. As I used to be DJ in disco clubs, I loved this place.

For years even before and after Wendy, I would rush out of work to go to this place after work. I worked an hour away. It was worth it to catch the last hour and then drive home or crash at the beach house if it wasn't occupied. We would go sometimes just for the weekends. After sunset, Wendy and I would go to a hotel or the beach house and relax, nap, have great sex and get ready for the night life. We would then party all night and crash. We would go home the next afternoon after finishing working on our tans. One night we spent the night in a motel that had walls so thin, you could listen to the conversation in the next room. One of these nights, the couple next door were having sex in a crappy bed, every room had one, with a poorly attached headboard and I swear we were there filming it. It was so loud. We had to wait until they stopped doing their thing to do our thing, as if that wasn't distracting.

7

Back to the regular routine, a few years has passed and everything seemed great. This was not so my friend. I don't know who became bored first. It's called the seven year itch. It can happen at any time. Wendy started to come home later and later after work from the bar until we were passing each other at 6:00am, me on my way out and her on her way home. That is when things started to fall apart. She loved cocaine so much that she needed to get that second job during the day to support her habit. It was a data entry job and the pay was alright. She admitted that the job was boring, as data entry was as boring then as it is now. To pass her time she told me she played with her nipples or her pussy to pass the time away. She was always the horniest woman I ever knew and she worked in a secluded room by herself. She was now working two jobs to support her lifestyle and she began to look tired all the time. I was getting concerned.

Now she was gone more and more, day and night just to feel the feeling. I never suspected that she had an addictive personality until much later in life, long after we were apart.

It started with Girls Night Out. This was an evening spent in the city with her girls friends until the wee hours of the morning. It was Thursdays as I recall and I trusted her, so I didn't have a problem with it. After a while I never became concerned when she came home the next morning, as this was becoming a regular practice for hers. I probably should have become suspicious but my heart was wide open and that was a mistake. After our sex life started to diminish, I realized something was up. Honesty was a trait in our relationship so I decided to open a can of worms to find out what was going on. She skipped right to the punch line and said she wanted her freedom and was going to move out. Let me fill in the blanks for you. There was a businessman who came to New York on Thursdays for business and Wendy would spend that night with him when he came to town. There were no girls in the Girls Night Out.

Ouch! I was hurt and young and figured that revenge was to be my reaction.

One night I was accused of cheating, which of course was not true. Working for a major hotel company, the budgeting process is an annual, lengthy and tedious process. This process is extremely time consuming, as in those days, there were no PC's, just calculators. There were meetings every week day and most weeknights for about eight weeks straight. Everytime the GM would change his mind or philosophies; we would have to re-crunch the numbers.

Many days we were locked in a room, so to speak, discussed the process, were given bathroom breaks, and ate Room Service for weeks. There were no cell phones back then, thank God, and I remember looking at my watch as it approached five o'clock wondering if we were going home anytime soon. The GM would look at our progress, the time table and the completion date and would make the call. This night like many others, was a night we were staying late. The GM would say, "Take 15 minutes and make your phone calls". I couldn't call Wendy at home as she was working day and night.

Getting home late at 2:00am, I got grilled by Wendy for having an affair just to get even. Trouble in paradise! This was fun. While I was locked in a meeting room, with flip charts, 14 column spread sheets and calculators, Wendy called the restaurant to talk to me. The Hostess told her she came in at three o'clock and hadn't seen me all day. Of course she hadn't seen me. This hotel was large and I parked in the hotel parking garage, so it's not like anyone would see my car and say, "he must be here somewhere, I saw his car". We were locked in this suite for almost two months and would really surprise people when we immerged from the room and appeared in the public spaces out of the blue answering the question "I didn't know you were here tonight"

So figuring like a stupid young person, I tell myself, if she can cheat and I am getting accused anyway, I might as well go for it. She's moving out and this relationship is probably coming to a close anyway. Looking at my options, I figured had a pretty good chance of scoring. I never had a problem getting laid back then, as I was considered a good catch. I had great respectable job, made great money and had lots of hair back then.

First was Susan, a waitress who worked for me and this breaks all the rules as one should not sleep with the hired help. She was always coming on to me and I decided I would pursue her. She lived a great distance away at some ski resort almost an hour away. Personally I would have moved closer. She lived with her parents, so she had no rent and gas was cheap so she stayed there. The first night her parents went out of town as they did a lot, she invited me over. This time I accepted. She made me a great dinner and we fucked like rabbits for hours. I love aggressive women. They assert so much effort that it is exhilarating as well as stimulating. Feeling a little guilty, I drove home thinking about Wendy and what she was doing and had done. I was trying to justify my actions. It took her what seemed like forever for her to move out, which made it harder for me to live with the guilt and being around her at the same time. I was never good at cheating and being okay with myself. My goal when I spent time with Susan was to get home before Wendy came home. Most of the time it worked. One night on my way home, it was winter and I blew the engine in my car. An old radiator hose ripped and all the little red lights came on. I decided that since it was three in the morning and snowing, I would try to make it. I did, got busted and had to spend $900 to get a used motor put in my car. What an expensive fuck. This affair went on for a while until I decided Jean, another waitress needed my help. She was unhappily married and needed some sex. I decided to help her out. Building up enough courage to perform this service I selected the right time frame when I knew Wendy would be at work for hours and set everything up. We went to our apartment and I brought Jean back to life. She had multiple orgasms before and during intercourse.

One night a few weeks later Wendy took a trip to go see her parents in Florida. This meant she would be out of town for a few days. I was seeking my next victim and it was the hostess. This was the blonde hostess who told Wendy she hadn't seen me all night when I was in budget meetings. She always came on to me and in the absence of Wendy I decided to have a small house party. I invited some friends as well as the hostess, Lisa. She was a big woman. Probably 5'10 with a large frame. She was young, maybe 20 but I wanted to do this just once. The party was a success and everyone left early, except Lisa. We had sex; I wouldn't call it making love, as I had no real feelings for her. This actually made it better. I have always been a lousy cheater as my conscience can't handle deception. I would rather be honest with my partner and more importantly myself.

Wendy, still hanging around and not making her move to relocate I become numb about my feelings for her. After our initial discussion about her cheating, she told me that one of the reasons she cheated on me was that I was no good in bed. She later told me she didn't mean this; she was just lashing out trying to be mean. Boy that hurt. At this point, I am not sure what she says is real or is influenced by her use of cocaine.

Next is yet another waitress, but not from my hotel. It's a woman I worked with in my training hotel an hour away. The assistant from that hotel, who I became friends with during my one month training, and later hired him as one of my assistant managers, decided he wanted to come, visit and party. He was bringing the girls. Working in a hotel in an executive management position gives you full access to the pool, the building and hotel rooms. Nice perk huh? He arrives with the girls and we go out for a while for drinks and then return to the hotel to continue the party. He takes off with his girl and Libbey and I are left chatting in my office. My office is a small hole in the wall just off the Lobby Bar. No windows, 2 desks and a lot of papers. I don't know how our conversation turned into a blowjob, but it did. After several cocktails and more cocaine we adjourned to a hotel room to have intercourse in the two beds with the two women. This was wild. In the same room with another couple makes this one for the books.

Wendy finally found an apartment nearby, not a good thing, and finally began to move. She had a roommate which financially made life easier. She never paid rent or any bills with me. She made plenty of money, worked two jobs, but still had that recreational habit. It can get expensive. After she moved out I became lonely and depressed, feeling bad about the affairs I had. I became immature and obsessed with her still, as I have always loved her and I began stalking her. It really didn't make any sense because after bird-dogging her from my car and from a tall tree outside her apartment I never saw her with anyone. This was stupid wasn't it? Still busy with my career, time seemed to pass without notice. One day a phone call from her turned into a visit. It was great to see her; she still looked tired as now the drug addiction is taking its toll. We refrained from having sex for a while as the hurt, the pain, and the cheating, was still too fresh.

She was always a wild thing as during one of my visits, which started to become a regular thing, she received a phone call and secretly dismissed the caller. I casually inquired and she actually explained the entire story to me. This guy, who called her, was calling a wrong number. This guy must have been a little dense as he kept calling. One day she decided to talk to this guy and it started a phone friendship. She didn't meet this turd until later. During one of her phone conversations with him she asked what he was doing. He said he had just gotten out of the shower. She asked him what he was wearing and he replied saying it was just a towel. She then asked him if his dick was hard and he said not yet. She continued to talk sexy to him until he was masturbating and had a full erection. Wendy then lay on her bed and the two of them engaged in phone sex resulting in mutual orgasms. She was a wild thing. I told you. One day I came over to her apartment to do some painting that the landlord refused to do as he didn't think it was necessary. While painting on a six foot ladder, wearing a pair of shorts and no shirt, Wendy performed another one of her infamous blowjobs while I was on the ladder. It was great until her roommate walked in and caught us. It was pretty exciting. Her roommate excused herself and went to her room. Wendy then finished the intended task. What a great roommate.

Life went on for both of us. I stopped keeping tabs on her as I didn't want to punish myself any longer. I got transferred a short while later to a hotel in Queens, New York. It was nineteen miles away so there was no need to move. The commute was a bitch however, I had to negotiate the city traffic and cross the George Washington Bridge and TheTriborough Bridge daily. It was 30-45 minutes in the early morning and over an hour during rush hour in the evening. The beauty of working so many hours in the hotel industry, you rarely went in or left during rush hour. I was usually in by seven in the morning and out by eight in the evening. Any time I was out early, I would drink at a bar across the street till the traffic cleared. I really hated bumper to bumper traffic. This new assignment was a challenge as well as a real bitch. The hotel was only open six months and three of my predecessors had already bailed. I was thrown to the wolves and I focused all of my waking time to overcoming this obstacle. I sort of put Wendy out of my mind as I was very busy.

A short time later she called me and wanted to see me and I agreed. I forget why she wanted to see me, but I didn't care as I really wanted to see her. We went out for dinner, had a nice time, and returned to the old apartment. Oh, the memories.

We did some cocaine and had some wine and screwed for the rest of the night. Gee it was great to see her again. No questions were asked and no statements were made, she just went home.

The commute to Queens was killing me so I decided to move to the city. I found a three bedroom condo in Bayside, which was perfectly located seven miles from the hotel and right on the Long Island Expressway (LIE). I had an assistant who also worked at the hotel and he was also looking to move so we became roommates. This was perfect as I worked 6:00am till 3:00pm and he worked from 3:00pm till closing. It was great because we never got in each other's way. Over time Wendy still came to visit. I was never sure if it was for the good cocaine or the good sex. I was hoping it was the latter. Time surged forward and we saw each other less and less. The emotions of our relationship seemed to have disappeared, but the sex was always great.

My Dad was dying of cancer and I would drive to Connecticut almost every week during his final days. When he finally passed away, I needed a big shoulder to cry on and I called Wendy and she was there for me. She took time off from both jobs and accompanied me to

Connecticut for the memorial services and the funeral. My family loved her as she had a huge heart, she was smart and regardless of everything that happened between us, she always loved me. She knew my Dad as we spent so much time at the beach house when he was there. Every night we slept together, whether it was during our time together or afterwards, it always felt so comfortable, as she had this amazing ability to relax me and make me melt away. This feeling has lived on forever.

 I lost touch with her now for some time and I received a disturbing phone message. She was behind three payments on her car. I began to wonder if her addiction had skewed her responsible attitude toward her financial obligations. I tried to call her but her phone was disconnected as apparently she had moved, (still no cell phones). The only lead I had was the data entry job she had during the day while working at Mandos. I called and she still worked there but was not currently there that day. I drove, on my next day off, to this place to get the creditors some information for them to help them collect this debt. Remember I co-signed the loan. I passed along the information and offered them a deal. I will make up the three payments she was behind if they would get me the car. It would be a simple repossession. However they did not know where the car was located. This was not a very efficient finance company if a little girl like Wendy could escape them that easily. This seemed to be an impossible task for them so it never happened. I never heard from them again nor did I hear from Wendy. It was a cool car too, a Black Camaro, t-tops, 5 speed, I could live with that. At the time I was just driving a shit box 1976 Monte Carlo.

8

Never hearing from her again, I moved on with my life. I don't know if she went home to the Midwest to rebuild her life or if she was still in town. All the time, I still did not know how serious her addiction was. I partied all the time and started my own little business as I had a little addiction problem now myself. I guess I have Wendy to thank for getting me hooked on this very expensive drug. The best way to pay for this is to become a dealer. It became a different and secret life of mine. My off duty life now consisted of meeting people in basements of bars and other strange remote places. I was always worried about getting busted and robbed so I carried a Colt 45 automatic mounted in a shoulder holster for protection. There were always tons of cash and tons of cocaine in my life. It was a normal thing for me to pick up an ounce every week and have $2000 cash on me at all times.

Wendy had faded from my life so I had to just go on living. I started dating a security guard at the hotel. Her name was Sherry. She was tall, 5'9", very attractive, large natural breasts and black. We had a lot of fun in those days. Some people were still hung up on interracial relationships. We got some looks, I'll tell you, especially when we were in public. Sherry had this cool stunt that she used to pull whenever we were in the car. A couple fitting the older, bigoted profile (Archie Bunker) would pull up alongside of my car and the man usually, and sometimes the wife, would look over and stare at us like one of us was an alien. Sherry would then lift up her top, press her tits up against the window and ask me to honk the horn. If just the husband was looking, this would get him in trouble as the wife would catch him looking at Sherry's boobs. I can't count the number of times we had fun with this one. Sherry and I had a great sex life, as we practiced five times or so per week. While I assumed my hotel responsibilities as Manager on Duty, a once a month duty of babysitting the hotel at night in the absence of the General Manager, it was usually a good night to get caught up on a project or some paperwork. For me it was a good night to help Sherry inspect some hotel rooms. She would obtain a list from the front desk with the status of every room. She would know which rooms were out of order, occupied or vacant. This would allow us to check the quality and comfort of the mattresses we were supplying our guests. It was kind of thrilling, if you think about it, the thrill of getting caught. We never did. She said she like having sex with white guys because while blacks were hung bigger, they rarely knew how to use it. I got no complaints from her.

I remember being so coked up one night on a Sunday when we were with my roommate and his date; we wanted to get some booze. The liquor stores were all closed and I resorted to my fellow bar operators/owners, to borrow a bottle until tomorrow. It was a fairly long search until I finally scored at a bar where I used to by my cocaine from a guy name Tippy. Really that was his name. We got a bottle of

Smirnoff and Sherry took it under her arm and protected with her life. After arriving at the condo, we proceeded to go inside. It was icy and had recently snowed and somehow, unbeknownst to anyone, Sherry dropped the bottle and it broke. That sucked!

Our relationship did not last very long and it had nothing to do with the vodka. One night after attending a movie in Queens, Sherry hustled me into an alley and released a sigh of relief. When I asked her what was up she it was her husband. Your Husband! The rest of the night we spent discussing her failing relationship with her spouse. I casually asked what is occupation was, she responded her was a New York City Detective. Great! This is not what I needed. I was dating a married woman of a New York City Detective who had a gun and a license to use it. My bigger concern other than dating his wife was my involvement with the drugs. No one would question a cop who shot and killed a drug dealer with product, cash and a weapon on him for a second. I broke off the relationship.

That went well for about a week. Then I met her Uncle Tony. I went to a bar near the hotel to pick up my usual ounce of cocaine and I was approached by a man. It was a short black man who reminded me of Sammy Davis Jr. He introduced himself as Tony and told me he was Sherry's uncle. He asked me to join him in his office so we could chat. So we went into the men's room and as he locked the door, I knew this didn't feel right. I decided not to overreact, kill anyone or break down any doors and just listen to him. He explained how Sherry's husband was a loser and it was a really big mistake for me to decide not to see her any longer. I explained that with my hobbies outside the company and her husband's occupation, it was not a smart decision to continue to see her. Next he took out a two gram vial of cocaine and used his fingernail as a spoon. This thing was custom grown. It was over an inch long and had a fricking shovel on the end of it. It was perfectly manicured. So as Uncle Tony proceeded to get me high as we continued to discuss his niece. With a half a gram up my nose by now, I did what all people do who are high on cocaine, I lied.

 People who are high on cocaine are never rational or think much, they usually just talk out of their ass. I wasn't quite sure what I was going to do next. My fear was that if Sherry's husband found out, it wouldn't take a genius how to figure out how to set me up, with his buddies, (I know a little about New York cops). It would be a justified shooting. Think about it, I always carried a gun and I always had cocaine and lots of cash on me. Pretty black and white no matter how you look at it. No pun intended, but it's there. I established a rule this day to only date officially divorced women. This did not include the ones thinking about it or going through it. It was the ones who were done with it.

I completed my transaction in the basement with Tippy. I ingested more happy powder as it is part of the business that you usually stay quite cooked most of the time. It amazing how I never missed a day of work in over thirty years and was never late. I was still high on occasion when I arrived at work, but we all know it was just adrenaline. I ignored Uncle Tony's suggestion and found a new source for my supply. That was a good move on my part although I had to travel to undesirable locations to acquire my product. Sherry called for a while and without cell phones, it was easy to ignore her calls. The answering machine was a great thing because you could decide who you wanted to call back, or not. She eventually went away and I never saw Uncle Tony again. I got transferred a short time later to Long Island, thank God, and now it was all behind me now. Sherry showed up at my new hotel one day a few months later, as it was not very far away. She was delivering something to the security office. I saw her for minute and we exchanged hellos, but that was it.

9

Before I left the airport property, I happened across two of the most beautiful women I had ever seen. They were from Miami. They were having breakfast and visiting on somebody's dime, I don't remember whose. I did a little research as I had contacts in the hotel. I saw that they had a suite and there were over one thousand dollars in charges in the hotel gift shop. Somebody had some money. They wanted to see the City. They asked several questions and it appeared to me that they were looking for a tour guide/chaperone. It is against the rules to date guests. I think you are getting to know me by now. I do bend the rules a little because it so much fun! I suggested that my roommate and I could take them into the City. We were in Queens and the City (Manhattan) was a hop, skip and a jump away. After explaining this to my roommate, also my assistant, he said he had plans. He was having dinner with his fiancée and didn't want to be put in a tempting situation. I understood and respect people who don't cheat on their respective other's when in a committed relationship. All this is happening in real time as the girls are still having breakfast. I explain to the girls that my roommate cannot come with us. I walk away to give them time to discuss the situation and upon my return, they asked if I could handle the two of them. Being young and confident I said "of course". We set a time and a place of pick-up, as discretion is of the upmost importance. People with no lives of their own, who could have witnessed me picking these girls up at the hotel, could have ended of my career. So we headed off to Manhattan.

We arrive at a famous Irish Pub and order some beers. After half of the first glass is gone, the girls don't waste any time asking if I knew where they could score some cocaine. I replied, "how about my right pocket". I said I always carried. I gave a small package to Karen and then she and Kelly went to the restroom. Returning with gleams on their faces I could tell they approved of the quality of the product and wanted more. I excused myself to go improve my own mood and to let the girls chat. Upon my return, the girls made some interesting suggestions. They first asked if I knew where I could get more cocaine. Then they hinted that we should get some liquor, Bombay, if I recall, and return to my house to party. My reply was, I don't live far away, I know where there is a liquor store open, and I have more cocaine than you will ever need. We departed the bar. We returned to the car and headed for a night I have never forgotten.

We stopped at a liquor store, picked up some gin. They didn't have Bombay and we had to settle for Tanqueray. We also got some tonic and some limes. We were set. On the ride home I gave Karen a kiss on the lips. It was sweet, but she commented that Kelly would be jealous. So she climbed over Karen and gave me a long wet kiss. This was going to be some night.

Finally arriving at the condo, my slacks are not fitting quite right, we enter the house. I put on some music and made some cocktails. The mood appears to be right and I broke out some more Happy Powder and we all indulged. The music played as the fish in the fish tank appear to be animated as we are now half cooked. The girls now want to dance. I'm okay with that as I love to dance. I am trying to evaluate the situation right now. I am with two beautiful girls who are from out of state. No-one knows them here so there are no reputations to ruin, except mine, so I guess anything could happen.

Thinking that this is going to be a threesome is a thought that always seems unrealistic, as this doesn't happen to many people. A ménage a trios is something most people only dream of. Remember I turned one down the first night I spent with Wendy with the Coffee Shop Sisters. I remain hopeful as my glass is always half full, not half empty. I am in good shape physically, usually in the gym three days per week so I can handle this easily if it happens. I am also in good shape physiologically. I have only had one beer in the City; I am on my first cocktail and I have only done about a half of gram of cocaine. I am going to pace myself because at this point I'm planning to go all night! The girls take a break and go to the bathroom together and return with a message for me. Karen explains to me that what is about to happen, never happened, and is never to be revealed or discussed again. She also stated that when it is over tonight, there will be no more contact, no phone calls, no emotion etc. Now I know, it's about to happen.

Karen and Kelly were both about five three. They were both about one hundred fifteen pounds and both had brown hair. They were from different ethnic backgrounds so their features were different. They were both very attractive and dressed very sexy. Sometimes the best part of a product is in its packaging!

We are all dancing on a dance floor we made by moving furniture in the living room and the girls want a striptease show. I complied. Mostly undressed at this point, I ask the girls to assist me with the balance of the show. Kelly comes to help with my request and upon removing the last piece of my clothing; she reveals an erection that is harder than the granite countertops in the kitchen. We move to the sofa and the sex begins. Karen begins a wonderful blowjob while Kelly plays with her pussy on the carpet. Karen and I switch places as I love to eat pussy. For thirty minutes this goes on and I can't stand it any longer. I have to have an orgasm soon or my balls are going to explode. We adjourn to the bedroom and foreplay ensues with both the girls. It was great. There were lips, licking, sucking, and kissing and body parts everywhere. It was the most erotic feeling I have ever had. I now penetrate Kelly and proceed to massage my dick with her pussy in several positions. Karen now experiencing a few orgasms of her own with Kelly coaching from the other side of the bed. It is time for my massive orgasm as I let it rip inside of her tight pussy, (no money shot here). A short break is in order as I am exhausted from this interlude. Kelly however, is in need of some relief so I help her out by performing cunnilingus on her until she has three orgasms.

Cocaine has multiple recreational uses. If you rub some on a woman's clitoris, it heightens the sensuality. We return to the living room for some more cocktails and more Happy Powder. We make small talk trying to pass the time as we were not supposed to communicate after this evening. Karen is a model for some magazine and Kelly is a wife of an illegal alien to allow him to become a citizen. She is paid a healthy allowance to keep her mouth shut and therefore just basically parties. She does not live with him so she is pretty well kept. An hour passes and we are ready for some more sex.

This was my first time receiving fellatio from two women at the same time. My penis has now recovered from our first session and is rock hard again. While enjoying my blow job I am now thinking of all the fantasies that I ever wanted or dreamed of. I felt as if any of my dreams were going to come true, tonight would be the night. I love to watch women masturbate so I made the suggestion. They complied without hesitation. Karen was on the couch and Kelly was on the floor. I explained that the objective was for everyone to give themselves an orgasm. I am now stroking my penis as they continue to excite me with their performances. Twenty minutes or so pass and everyone achieves an orgasm including the money shot this time. Another break is in order. More cocktails and Happy Powder are consumed. A few hours have now passed and my sick perverted mind reveals another fantasy. All men like to watch girl on girl action. I make the suggestion but they are reluctant to do this at this time. They suggested maybe later. I just realized that no one has eaten any food. You know what, no one was hungry. Cocaine does that to you. That why all the coke junkies are skinny, they don't eat.

I am ready for more sex now as another hour has passed. I felt that it was unfair that I didn't have intercourse with Kelly and that it was time. I asked Karen if she would help me stimulate her during this process and she said, absolutely. We joined Kelly on the floor and I proceeded to prepare her pussy by licking, kissing and massaging it with my tongue. I asked Kelly to get on top as this is one of my favorite positions. As she mounted me I asked Karen to sit on my face so I could eat her pussy. She complied. With the two girls now facing each other they began to kiss. First the kissing was light pecking and as they seemed to enjoy it. They intensified their passion and were now going at it tongues and all. This aroused me even more as Kelly was riding me like a bull at Giley's night club. Forty minutes now passes as it becomes harder and harder for men to orgasm during the heavy use of cocaine. We consumed about a total of four grams that night. At street value, it was about a four hundred dollar night. It was well worth it. Now after having my third orgasm, (there was no Viagra back in the eighties), the girls needed some relief and to my amazement they decided, that since I was shot, they perform cunnilingus on each other. All my dreams were coming true tonight. Experiencing more orgasms and producing big smiles, I think we are about done for the night.

It's now three in the morning and six hours with these girls has passed and it's time for one last cocktail and one last line. This was a great nightcap to an unforgettable evening. I still remember the date, even if it was almost thirty years ago. You would remember too, I'm almost sure, if it happened to you. We departed the condo and headed for the car so I can take the girls back to the hotel. More kissing and residual passion fills the car as this night is coming to an end and will only be a personal memory after this. I discreetly park a block down the street, something you pick up when you deal drugs, and we kiss good night and it is now over. Boohoo. I return home with a grin on my face and a smile on my penis.

I return home and decide to have a beer and smoke a cigarette. Thank the Lord; I don't have to work tomorrow or today. My roommate is home now and he has a puzzled look on his face. I ask him what is wrong and he says, "look". I ask him to look at what? He says the place is a wreck and it smells like SEX. I said "it should" and I explained the story to him. Now let me paint a picture for you. All the furniture in the common areas has been moved, there is evidence of cocaine use on the kitchen counter, the bathroom sink, the glass dining room table, and the marble coffee table. The dance floor is still in place and it does smell like sex. I told him he should have come with us, but I completely understand. As I said before, I respect people who honor their relationship and do not cheat. I however, was not in a committed relationship. It amazed me because even after seeing the evidence that was present, he still did not believe me. After all, it is a pretty incredible story.

A few months goes by and I am told a have a phone call that I have to take. I ask who it is and the messenger says "they didn't say". Remember the eighties. There are no cells phones, no caller ID, and no internet. So I take the call. You'll never guess who it was, so I will tell you. It's Karen! Wow, what a surprise. To my amazement, she wants me to come and visit her in Fort Lauderdale. She had a shoot there and wanted me to come and spend some time with her. Well now this would be breaking her rule of never seeing each other again. Hey, everyone breaks rules, especially me. I have broken other people's rules or organizations rules, but have never broken any of my own rules without good cause. Everyone has rules. Gibbs, (NCIS) has a whole set of rules and they are actually numbered. So Karen is going to break one of her rules. Oh well. I have a lot of vacation time built up as my company can never seem to grant requests for vacations and time always accrues. As a department head with this company, you never lose your vacation time as with some companies. At one point I had twelve weeks in the bank. So I decided to take some time and go visit her. I told myself it couldn't hurt. So I requested time off, got approve and booked a flight and a hotel room and was on my way to sunny Florida.

I usually vacationed to Florida and points south as being stuck in New York; it was always nice to go some place warm in the wintertime and work on my tan. It made people jealous when you returned to work. The beauty of working for a major hotel company was that hotel rooms anywhere were either free or cheap depending on occupancy. I had an assistant manager once whose wife worked for an airline. His rooms and his flights were cheap. He went some really cool places, sometimes just for the weekend. I arrived at the airport in Fort Lauderdale and there is a guy with a little sign with my name on it. I approach him and he asked me to come with him as he was my transportation. I had arranged for a rental car but decided to pick it up at the hotel. We walk over to a huge stretch white limousine, which was sent from the shoot by Karen for me. I thought this was really fantastic as I was feeling kind of special right now. I arrived at the shoot and Karen was working. After the shoot the limo took us to my hotel. I unpacked and we made arrangements to meet for dinner and whatever would follow. The limo took her back to the house she was staying at and I picked up my rental car. I came prepared as I brought plenty of cash, credit cards and of course, cocaine. Security in airports back then was pretty much nonexistent. You could get almost anything on a plane except an Uzi.

I picked her up for dinner and we ate at a place of her choosing. Dinner was good. I was feeling good as I hadn't had a vacation in a while and it was just great to get away. After dinner Karen wanted to party so we went to a night club not too far away. Night clubs in Fort Lauderdale are awesome. This place was three stories, two bandstands on different levels, which provided continuous entertainment and a Jacuzzi on the third floor where clothing was optional. I knew something was wrong when we entered the nightclub and the bouncers refused to admit her. There was some discussion about something that happened the last time she was there. WTF! I smoozed the bouncer into letting her in as I told him she would be under my supervision. He waffled for a bit and let us in. She wanted some cocaine and I had left mine in the room thinking we were going back there after dinner. She said she knew a source that was there and if I would give her some cash, she could score for us. I made a good living and had lots of money, dealing drugs is very profitable if you don't get high on your own supply. I said what the hell. I gave her over one hundred dollars and off she went. She returns in a few minutes and tells me she has to take a short trip to go pick up the score. I kiss her good-bye and begin to enjoy myself in this awesome atmosphere. After an hour or so has passed, I become a little concerned. I have no feelings for this woman as the one night was just that, one night. My concern was for my hostess who invited me for the weekend. Another half an hour has passed and she finally returned. Her pupils were so dilated that you couldn't tell what color her eyes were. She was fucked up. When I asked her where the cocaine was she said it was gone. Now that I'm pissed that one hundred and twenty five dollars of my money is gone, I start the inquiry. She starts going on about she did coke with this guy and he tried to rape her, yada, yada, yada. We left the club and went back to the place she was staying. This trip is not starting out as one of my favorite vacations. We arrive and I think what a dump. She is staying with a friend and this shack does not appeal to me at all. So we head back to my hotel. She grabbed a joint for us to smoke on the way there and finally I feel that I am back in control and in my comfort zone. I figured that there would be hours of sex followed by some well deserved jetlagged sleep. Boy was I wrong. No sex was the message that she made crystal clear. I did not come all the way to Florida to watch her get high on my dime and not at least get laid. She crashed and spent the night and I took her home in the morning. With only four days of vacation, the first one was not too great. She was working a half day the next day, so I told her I would pick her up at the shoot. We went to lunch at the hotel pool bar and up to the room for an afternoon delight. I practically had to force myself on her. It was not enjoyable at all.

At this point I am not sure what is going on but Karen, obviously a coke whore, has a more serious problem than I thought. Anything to get high and fuck everything and everybody else. Ouch!! I took her home and as she had some *things* to do? I told her I was going to go to the beach and work on some well needed rest and my tan. As I returned to the hotel I broke out in an immediate sweat. The parking lot of the hotel was loaded with Sherriff's Department cars. This reminded me of the movie of the movie Bonnie and Clyde or Butch Cassidy and the Sundance Kid. I really didn't think I was a big enough dealer to require all this attention. I had maybe ten grams of cocaine in my room. I decided this collection of law enforcement vehicles was not for me so I entered the hotel. I was right. Upon entering the hotel I looked at the reader board in the lobby, displaying the banquet events of the day and there was a Florida Sherriff's Convention being held at the hotel this weekend. I issued a sigh of relief.

She said she would call me later. Several hours had past and finally she called my room with an awesome suggestion. She wanted to go to the Florida Keys to hang out with her Uncle Ray for the rest of the weekend. The Florida Keys was a four hour drive. At this point my expectations of this weekend were totally skewed. I thought about it for a while and what I wanted to do for the rest of the weekend and made a decision. I figured the next three days would be similar to the last day. I called the airline and changed my ticket. I decided to go home. I was not having any fun. Karen was to be dropped off at my hotel by a friend, (suspicious of that too) and we were driving to the Keys. She left a few articles of clothing and some sundries behind, so I greased the maid and left the items with her to give to Karen when she arrived, as I was departing for the airport. I would rather go home and shovel snow up my nose and out of my driveway then spend one more minute with Karen. Arriving back in New York I decided to chill for the next few days. I had made a grave mistake going to visit her. My expectations

and the memory of that one night
did not realize my idea of seeing her
again. We never spoke again.

10

Getting transferred is sometimes a good thing because you can leave stuff behind. I have left a lot of women behind as well as some unwanted habits. When I was transferred to Long Island I left the dealer shit behind me.

Now I was just into picking up an eight ball once or twice a week. I guess you could say I curtailed my habit. Still living in Bayside, it was now time to move. We found a house, three bedrooms and a loft and I had three roommates. One was the old roommate, living on the first floor and Tom who was a kitchen guy who occupied the first floor as well. Kevin lived upstairs in the loft and I lived in the basement with a fully functional kitchen and bathroom. It was a sweet place. Life zoomed by as the challenges in Long Island were great as well. I earned the reputation as the "Fix-it Guy". If the company had a hotel with a problem that no one could fix, they sent me. This house was an Animal House of sorts as there was always someone over partying, snorting, drinking and having sex. I can't remember how many trips we made to White Castle to grab 50 cheeseburgers, fries and milkshakes to cure the munchies.

Roommates are a subject for a different book as there are always situations that need attention. There are rules when living with roommates. Never take the last of anything. That means the last beer, the last swig of booze, the last joint or the last line. These things never seem to work out. Working in Long Island's most popular bar, there were lots of nights that I would get home after 4:00am. All the booze was gone, my private stash of Jack Daniels consumed and the liquor stores were closed. This wasn't working out so I resorted to padlocks, just so I could have something to drink when I got home to relax. Backgammon became an obsession in this house as everyone played and it was not unusual for a game to be in progress every night I came home. It is a game I still enjoy.

I met my next wife who was a Recreation Supervisor at the hotel. I worked out regularly and always have throughout my entire life. Our relationship developed and we ended up getting married. As I look back, this was another mistake in my life. Our sex life was pretty different as she was a virgin and stayed that way until our wedding night. Our sex life before we got married consisted of manual and oral stimulation. This was fairly satisfying to both of us. There was no intercourse until the wedding night. On that wedding night, in the Cayman Islands, it was an uncomfortable experience for both of us and neither one of us enjoyed it. I know you find it hard to believe, but it was true. I think my expectations were too high. Hence forth, the disappointment was a tragic reality. I guess it's like buying a motorcycle and not being able to take it for a test drive. Then you get the bike and drive it home and it is not what you expected. With all my experience I tried to teach her and clone her into someone who enjoyed sex, but it never developed. I don't think she ever wanted to learn. It was not the right time for her to tell me after we got married. That's why people have pre-marital sex, to test drive it before making the commitment. It reminded me of my high school sweetheart. After dating for two years, it was the same kind of sexual relationship. The only difference was we never had intercourse.

II

Wendy and I both went our separate ways and a lot of things happened to both of us while we were apart. There were marriages, children, addictions and relationships that occurred. All these things we found out later after we got back together. It just fits better in this book so you can understand the backgrounds of both of us and what we went through to get to the next point in our lives together.

Wendy went on and got married and had three children. I had got married twice more. My oldest son from my first marriage grew up to be a fine young man. He graduated college, got married and has a successful life of his own.

I am not one to criticize why marriages don't work as I have no room to talk. I really believe that a couple should have to answer a 200 question profile questionnaire and a judge should approve or disapprove it before issuing a marriage license.

It would be just like some dating websites to see if you are compatible. They (divorces) are almost always ugly when they end and eventually you become friends. Wendy told me that. She and her ex-husband were best friends. I never believed it would happen to me. Eventually it did.
I got transferred to Manhattan for nine months to do an opening and then to St Louis, Missouri. I took my second wife as I was not one to be languid and give up. I had faith.

In the years Wendy and I were apart there were a host of other problems too. Addiction was the most prominent one in Wendy's life. It started with the cocaine and the alcohol was always there. She partied hard for years before she decided to settle down. We know that addicts are ALWAYS addicted to something. Alcoholics quit drinking and get addicted to coffee. Cocaine users get addicted to better shit, and I don't know what sex addicts get addicted to after they quit. Maybe they become addicted to drugs and alcohol. If you're ever looking for an alcoholic, go to

Starbucks at eleven-thirty at night and they will be there drinking coffee. Addicts can't handle life without a buffer. They always have to find something that helps them to cope. I know a few people addicted to Facebook. I know some people addicted to their phones. The ability for people to manage social skills amazes me. I see people who cannot or will not talk to you until they get off their phones. I know people who are late for work because they have to check their Facebook for ten minutes before going to work. Wake up early, what a thought!

Wendy was addicted to sex, as well. When we were together that was fine because I was with her. I believe that her addiction is why she moved out and left me. As you may recall, she still had sex with me after we broke up. A little bird told me once that Wendy used to slightly exaggerate some of her relationship stories. Her addiction to drugs became even worse after she finished school and became an RN. Now she had access to the good stuff. She could get her hands on all kinds of pain killers including Morphine. Ouchh! She would shortchange her patients on their full dosage so she could get high and stay high. She went as far as going in on her day(s) off, not for the extra money, but to get high. She told me she did some unbelievable things which I will not share with you. Sorry. She was thrown in rehab twice and lost the custody of her children because of this problem. This was a very expensive lesson.

My problem was a little different. I lost the cocaine habit when I got transferred to Manhattan. I remember one night my co-worker, Jack and I went out drinking one night in the City to a place where he said it was so cool there, you could do lines of coke right there on your mirror top cocktail tables. I trusted Jack, but he was wrong because as soon as we laid out a few lines we met the bouncers. Three gentlemen about six foot four inches and over two hundred pounds. They told us we were misinformed. We apologized and went to the rest room and decided to use the stalls to shuffle the coke back and forth under the walls to get high but the same three bouncers came in and stopped that party as well. Eventually they tossed us out. Thanks Jack!

There was a different crowd of people I hung out with and this was not a nightclub atmosphere like in Long Island. I just quit one day with no help at all. There were no side effects or withdrawal. I guess I wasn't physically addicted. I began to drink a lot more and that became my biggest addiction. I didn't drive as I used mass transit in and out of the city. There was no harm to me or others as I was not behind the wheel. I got transferred to a St Louis property after nine months and the problem came with me. The problem now is I was driving. It is a strange concept that the more people drink on a daily basis, they can actually function when they are legally drunk. My problem with my addiction was also access. I had the keys to all the liquor storerooms and bars. I could access anything at anytime if I was smart, and I was. It got so bad one day when I was on my way to the Chiropractor, I hit one of those concrete dividers on the interstate. When my BMW bounced off it back into the highway, I woke up. It was two in the afternoon. I also passed out once with my face dropping into my entrée plate. I blamed work for most of my problems as things were impossible. I had a boss who felt threatened by my presence as I was more qualified to do his job than he was. He did everything he could to make me quit or get fired. He berated my assistant managers to a point where most of them quit. Instead of replacing them he made the two remaining mangers work all the shifts. I was the morning manager and I work seven days a week from five in the morning until nine in the evening. The other manager came in at noon and worked until closing, seven days a week. Whenever I complained, he just said that there weren't any candidates available and he just rode me harder. He gave me more paperwork (senseless projects) and performed stupid things like sanitation inspections. Eventually I gave in and I left the company after eight years.

He hired four managers after I gave my notice. I thought there were no candidates! I move to Florida to open my own restaurant. When I left St.Louis, I left the bottle behind. I still think it must have been stress related as I have never been in rehab and I have never gone to an AA Meeting. I never touched another drop of liquor ever again. However I do enjoy beer and wine from time to time, but I know the dangers of addiction.

A silly fact is that I was in St. Louis, Missouri while Wendy was in Kansas City, Missouri at the same time. Hmmm?

12

I opened a New York style delicatessen as getting a decent sandwich in this state was a real task. There were no Blimpies or Subways and supermarkets like Publix didn't make sandwiches until much longer after I opened my restaurant. They didn't even sell Boar's Head cold cuts to any supermarkets until a few years after I closed. They were keeping the "Deli Quality" thing sacred. It was a thirty seat deli with a large display case full of fresh made salads. I was using recipes from a New York deli that I obtained from a friend who ran a deli in Long Island. There was the classic New York Style potato salad as well as three other potato salads, the classic New York Style cheesecake and cool things like bagels and knishes. There were no bagel shops in this town either when I arrived. So I did quite well.

I divorced my second wife as the whole relationship never developed forward it just seem to go in reverse. I loved sex and without it I wasn't happy. We grew apart and got divorced and went our separate ways. There was no property and no children, so it was just a little paperwork that needed to get done. Needing to have some sex as I have now gone faithfully without sex for almost five years. Having really great sex had been even longer. Remember what I said about cheating. You are greatly respected by everyone if you don't cheat and you wait until the ink of the divorce paperwork has dried. I'm sorry but I liked sex too much to live without it, as that part of our lives diminished early and never recovered.

I started dating Debbie. She was five-nine, had blonde hair and beautiful blue eyes. She was a customer and I didn't have to worry about breaking any rules as I owned the place. She worked in a store in the mall I was in and she was a regular customer. After she learned of my divorce, she came on to me. I played it out and we began dating. We had something in common. She loved sex. This worked out great as it seemed like that is all we ever did. I think one of her goals was to see if it was possible to wear out the sex organs. We had sex everywhere. We would have sex in the restroom at the deli after lunch slowed down. We did it standing up as she was tall enough to make that fairly easy. It was just an afternoon delight to take the edge off the stress of my day. The craziest place we ever did it was in a Jacuzzi in someone's condominium complex.

I knew someone who used to live there so I knew the location of the Jacuzzi. It was in a remote location on a canal. The condos were between us and the street so it provided perfect cover. It was later in the evening, about ten and we parked and went in the hot tub. Debbie was a little concern, or should I say paranoid as she just smoke a joint. She said if someone sees us they will call the police. I said how they would know from a distance that we didn't live there. The nearest condo was about one hundred feet away and it was dark. She agreed. Debbie proceeded to remove the bottom of her bathing suit so she could let the hot tub water jets stimulate her clitoris. I enjoyed watching her being stimulated until she finally reached an orgasm. Now that I have an erection, Debbie decides it my turn. After I tried the jet stimulation thing, I wasn't as successful. Debbie than came over to assist as she proceeded to perform an "Up Periscope Blowjob". It was also exciting because we could see the condos from a distance. Knowing people were able to see us, weather they did or not, was still pretty exciting.

Debbie and I started to have problems when her love of drugs became a bigger part of her life than I was. In the beginning, it was all about the newness of the relationship and constant sex. Our relationship should have had some friendship components to it as well as the sex, but it didn't. It became a problem when after she began getting to know my staff and their love of smoking pot, they became friends. I am not sure who she spent more time with her after a while, me or my staff. I was cleaned up at this time and no longer used cocaine or drank liquor. I smoked an occasional joint now and again, but it was rare. One night I wanted to take Deb out to dinner and she wanted to stay home. I asked what was up and she said she had some friends coming over. I told her we had made plans two days ago and that it wasn't fair to me to change those plans at the last minute. I asked her who was coming over and you quest it, my pot smoking staff.

I am assuming this relationship doesn't have much life left to it so I decided to join in the fun. I stopped by her house. I didn't smoke as I was going to play golf with my brother the next day, so I needed to stay sober. I was scheduled to leave to travel to the golf course at six in the morning. The tee time was sevenish. I hung out and felt very out of place as everyone in the room was screwed up except me. Everyone had dropped acid and the world was different for all of them but not me. Keeping with my intended schedule, I decide to go to bed and crash at Debbie's house. Son of a Bitch. Somebody drop a hit of acid in my drink. I had never been there before so now I am tripping all night and wake up with something that felt a lot worse than my worst hangover. My head is pounding. If feels like it is stuck under a truck tire. Now I am suppose to play golf in this condition. However there is one thing I need to do first before I leave. I tell Debbie you can hang out with my staff all you want, but we are DONE!! I don't know who spiked my drink and I don't really care. Somehow drugs are always messing up my life.

A short time later some regular customers come in for lunch with someone I had never seen before. Her name was Jodi. She was five-eight, brown hair, dyed blonde, with big brown eyes. I love brown eyed girls. She was young and gorgeous. I asked my friend who she was and she said she was just a friend. I asked about her and she didn't really know too much about her personal life. Later Jodi called her and she was asking about me. Apparently she was interested. My friend told me the news and dropped me her phone number. Wow, I was pumped. I made the call. She was ten years younger than me and that didn't seem to matter to her. We went on our first date and all I could do was stare at her and fanaticize. I wanted to do things to her that would make her want me forever. On our first date I invited her over for dinner at my apartment. After dinner, which I cooked for her, we shared some wine. Now we're relaxing on my bed and I make my move. We start kissing (so sweet) and touching and this becomes quite sensual. I eventually removed her jeans and needed to see if she was as sweet on the inside and she was on the outside. Eating a young pussy for dessert was just what I had in mind. She didn't fight, resist or try to stop me. She just laid back and enjoyed what was about to come. It was great and it became the hook in our relationship.

She quickly moved in as her current living situation had fallen apart. I questioned her motive on our first date as she needed a place to live NOW! I woke her every morning with oral sex until she had an orgasm and then she would mount me and ride me until I achieved a smile that would last me all day. She was a unique and special girl as I loved her frugal style of living. She would go to secondhand stores, Goodwill, Salvation Army, etc., and buy me the coolest clothes. She would spend $3.00 on a Polo shirt and the same for jeans. She said I didn't dress very "hip" after my divorce. So she bought me lots of clothes for next to nothing. The first night we went out she came out of the bedroom to show me a pair of jeans she had bought. She asked me if I liked them and I hesitated. She went back in the bedroom and came out with a denim skirt on 30 minutes later. I loved the skirt and told her I did. She said it used to be those jeans I just had on. Talented girl with a needle and thread.

Our relationship consisted of spending time at the beach. Her dad had a beach house nearby, fifteen minutes, and we would spend time there. Jodi was a little daring, as one time she removed her bottom of her swimsuit and climbed aboard when we were in the water. We stayed that way for a while until we both had orgasms. It was exhilarating having sex and watching all those people on the beach looking at us not know what we were really doing. After all it was the middle of the afternoon on the weekend. The beach was pretty crowded. My favorite memory of Jodi was fulfilling her dream of having oral sex while listening to her favorite music wearing her headphones. So I surprised her one night and scored some pot from a buddy of mine and bought some rum, as Jodi liked rum and coke. When she got home from work, the mood was set. The lighting was perfect and I was ready to fulfill a fantasy of hers. She walked in and could see pillows and a comforter on the living room floor. She noticed the rum and the pot. She knew what was about to happen. She went and got her music, we had a drink and smoked a joint and now we are ready. She laid back and removed all her clothes. I went to work. Remember that Jodi had on headphones so I could not hear the music. My performance was based on the reactions of her body. When she came close to orgasm, I would stop or change the rhythm of what I was doing. This would postpone the orgasm, but more importantly intensify it. I spent close to an hour on this project and the results were outstanding. The intensity of her orgasm was amazing as her whole body trembled and shuttered as she came.

Our relationship was based mostly on sex. I would say I loved being with her and she always looked good on my arm, but I was not "in love" with her. She wanted to go see an old boyfriend once. Here we go with the big slong theory. She said his penis was twelve inches long and provided a sensation that I could not provide and it enabled more sexual position than men somewhat less endowed could. I am not sure she ever slept with him again although I know she did go and see him at work one day.

She went off in a different direction when she starting dating the owners son where she worked. They had rules. They secretly snuck around.

He was younger (than me) and she explained that they experienced "the touch". I know you have heard of love at first sight but have you ever heard of or experienced "the touch"? If you have experienced it than you know what I mean. If you haven't I will explain. When you are with someone for the first time and you feel an attraction that is one thing. But, when you touch for the first time and you get all kinds of sensations. Your heart may skip a beat or stop for a second or you may experience a tingling sensation throughout your entire body. That is "the touch". Jodi had this feeling with him and not me and I was okay with that as I told you I was not in love with her. I would just move on. Their relationship fell apart after a short while, as the rules got in the way. It was a family business and he was the owner's son and you know what I said about rules.

After Jodi decided to leave and move back home to Arkansas, we decided on a peaceful ending. I even drove her and her Jeep back home as we broke up and I flew home. During her final weeks I granted her one last request. She wanted to do some cocaine with me before she left. I hadn't done this in quite some time but I agreed and scored two grams for our extended farewell party. We still had lots of sex as it was always fun and very enjoyable for both of us. One day we got home from a trip to the beach early, maybe two o'clock in the afternoon and she told me "I am going to make your dick hard and keep it that way all day and all night". I didn't argue. (*Use your imagination to complete this paragraph).*

I made the trip to Arkansas and we had great sex on the day I left. I again would get on with my life. I cried on the plane half way home and I don't know why. Remember, I was NOT in love with her. However another faux pas occurred with my travel arrangements as my ticket home was confirmed from Fayetteville. The problem was I was in Arkansas and the ticket was for Fayetteville, North Carolina. I got home after eight hours and visiting Dallas and Atlanta.

I eventually would close the Deli as things changed. One mall anchor moved out and the other anchor went out of business. Subway has moved in close by and MacDonald's has opened up across the street. After three years it was time to move on. The economy was strong back then and retail lease rates were extremely high, so I decided to close up and find a job and go back to work. That's where I met Jennifer. I am working as a Sauté Chef at a waterfront restaurant on one of Florida's keys. It's a night time position and the pay isn't that great but at least I am getting a paycheck every week unlike owning your own business where you pay yourself, what you can, when you can. There is a feisty little blonde working there who wore the shortest shorts I have ever seen on a waitress. I set my sites on her and really wanted to have sex with her. I finally invited her to the beach to split a bottle of wine with me. She agreed and upon returning to her place, good old sex happened. She especially loved to way I stimulated her pussy with my tongue, as I figured you guessed by now, it was one of my favorite things to do with women. She was a horny woman and that was right up my alley.

She had a night time job working as a cocktail waitress which was located past my house. She had to drive by my house after work to get to her house. Frequently she would stop by my house after work which usually was pretty late. The bar closed at two and then there was the clean up and then there was the two or three shift drinks and then she would arrive at my house. Three or four in the morning was her typical arrival time. I worked nights so I didn't really care. Most night she woke me up by climbing into bed with me and performing oral sex on me until I woke up. I gave her a key. She always insisted that I give her oral orgasms. She used to say before I left her house or before she left mine, just one more. Of course I complied. She also gratefully returned the favor with oral sex and used the prolonged orgasm method which I loved and hated at the same time. Hated the waiting but I loved the outcome.

This relationship didn't last but a few months as I found out how much she liked sex. I thought something was suspicious when she would never see me on a Friday night. That's because she was seeing a guy I knew that I played softball with. He would have sex with her on Friday and I would always see her on Saturday. Not anymore.

Now that relationship was over there was only one more relationship before I got married for the third time. Her name was Debbie, I know, another Debbie. Hey I don't pick the names, I just write about them. She was the night bartender and we had worked together for a few years. She asked me why I had never asked her out. I didn't have an answer so we went to dinner. A relationship developed and I eventually asked her to marry me. The sex wasn't that great but I figured I needed to settle down a bit anyway. So I figured I would make some sacrifices. After all I think I have had about enough sex to last me a lifetime anyway. Now that we are engaged, the late night after bar shit really needed to stop. She had a thirteen year old son who was living with us now and I didn't appreciate Debbie not being home by seven o'clock in the morning to make him breakfast and get him off to school. I did it for a while and soon got tired of it. I just let him sleep in and miss school. I would let Debbie explain to the school board why her son was missing so much school. He was not my child, but if you are out snorting cocaine with your buddies while I am raising your kid, I draw a thick dark line in the sand. She wouldn't stop her late night or early morning, I should say, habits. She just came up with more lame excuses. Working on a key lends you to unfortunately sometimes use as an excuse the bridge malfunctioning but not as much as she used it. I used to call the city the next day to see if the bridge had really malfunctioned and of course I was right. I told you people on cocaine lie a lot. This wasn't working and I had to end it, so I did. By the way she to this day is still with this cokemeister. I don't know what happened to her son and I don't really care.

I have not seen or heard from or thought of Wendy in almost ten years now.

Moving on to my next marriage. I got married again to my third wife and had a lovely son. Now I am raising a second family hoping to spend more quality time with my second son than I did my first one. Watching him grow, doing homework with him and just being with him everyday made me happy. There is not much to say. I speak a lot about it in the next chapter as to why it didn't work. The whole background as to how it started and progressed over the next fifteen years has no bearing on this story. So I will not waste your time on the subject.

I was working for a different hotel company for five years and politics got involved and I lost that battle. I also got a DUI after a visit from my brother led us to a watering hole where I spouted off too much about my ex-wife and consumed too many glasses of Pinot Noir.

13

Now divorced for the third time, I have just moved out of my house from my third ex-wife and I am living in a rented house by myself and my two dogs. While being unemployed, and financially recovering from the cost of a DUI, my life is looking pretty sad, no matter how you look at it. My divorce is not final as my attorney is holding the final decree hostage until my unpaid balance of thousands of dollars is paid. My attorney got a postponement, great. Wendy had the same rule about dating almost divorced people. I have always been financially creative. I rented this house while unemployed and even bought I car while unemployed once. It's all about credit score.

I am doing some volunteer work at a local non-profit organization to satisfy my community service hours, got my car impounded for ten days, some stupid law passed my MADD (Mothers Against Drunk Drivers) causing me to rent a car with, more money I don't have. I see my fifteen year old son two days a week as ordered by the court. Life seems pretty bleak and my self esteem diminishes. Due to the divorce and my DUI, I am now thirty thousand dollars more in debt than I was a year ago. While still looking for a job I begin to sell things around my house of great value. These are just some things I have lugged around for years as we all do. Some of the items have some value and I have to raise enough cash to pay my attorney. The process goes well and I am finally able to pay off my attorney and get my Final Decree. I am now a free man. Now I just have to pay off my DUI lawyer and the associated cost costs.

Things start to look up as the non-profit now offers me a job after completing my community service as they like the way I work. It's hard work for a man my age, now 54, but it's a job so I accept. This job includes cleaning and preparing donated appliances to get them ready for resale. So I am now scrubbing toilets and scrubbing major appliances, which have not been cleaned in certain places in a while. Going from my last job @ $73,000 a year to ten dollars an hour is beyond tough. I keep my head as high as I can but I am clearly not making it. I have never been one to give up or just quit anything, including life itself. I persist. I have child support to pay, rent, food etc and this job isn't cutting it. I search for a part time job at night and I remembered that a friend and former colleague of mine just opened a restaurant. I went to visit him and told him my situation. He agrees to hire me and I am now working there two nights a week as a waiter and Sunday for breakfast and lunch. The money is not bad and I start to pull myself out of the very deep hole I am in. I am however still depressed as I have no life except the little time I spend with my son. He is, as all children are when their parents get divorced, pissed at both of us. It's a constant challenge as they always think that their parents will get back together. I attend a parenting class, required by the court, which was actually very informative. I couldn't wait for my soon to be ex-wife to take the same class. It straightens you out about how to treat each other and how to especially treat your children.

After arriving home from work and a long day of hard labor, I walk outside to pick up my mail and there is a letter in my mailbox that was forwarded from my old address. It was from Wendy, **_twenty seven years later_**. Wow! I don't open it immediately as my mind is like a scrambled egg right now, whipping around memories and the incredible idea that this could be true. I convince myself that since it is addressed to me I should open it. I couldn't read it fast enough or enough times to completely digest the message. It starts out pretty much like "I hope this letter finds you well". She goes on to apologize in the event she is interrupting my wonderful life (if she only knew) and says she doesn't want to cause any problems if I am happy. She goes on to explain what she has been doing for the last twenty-seven years, her marriages, her three wonderful children and the associated custody and living arrangements. She is working as a

Registered Nurse in Kansas City, Kansas, making good money and enjoying life.

She asked what I had been up to, and began to explain how she had researched my life via the internet before writing this letter. She knew where I had worked. As when I was in management, I was frequently listed in press releases for assignments or promotions. She obtained my address from the internet as well as my phone number. She said she felt uncomfortable calling, as if my wife or children answered the phone, she might not know what to say. I was impressed to say the least as twenty-seven years ago, there was no internet and she was just a young cocktail waitress whom I was in love with once. The only research anyone did back then was in your local library. She gave me her email address and asked me to email her to update her on my life. She started her letter by saying she had been thinking about me lately. I couldn't say the same but now I will be sleepless until I respond. My scrambled mind is now an omelet as there is so much going through my mind. "What could she possibly want?" She didn't leave me a phone number but there was a return address on the letter if I opted to write instead. She said she would understand. I put the letter away and recorded her email address in my contacts list as I needed time to think of an appropriate response. I didn't want to sound depressed and didn't want to come off as the loser I was feeling like lately. The last time she saw me I was a successful executive manager for a major hotel company. Now that I was nothing, I was trying to think of a way to tell her I was between careers or jobs or something. I needed to sleep on this. (Huh) It was not likely that any sleeping was going to happen this night. My mind was a racetrack but I was very, very happy to hear from her. Every once in a while, everyone needs a life changing event in their life and this was mine!!!

At first I wondered if this was just a friend checking up on a friend or if she was coming to town to see her parents and wanted to see me. I had no idea. I also figured she dumped me way back when and I'm sure she would not think we would ever get back together again. Hopefully she figured out I would never forgive her for breaking up with me. I went to sleep thinking this would be a pen pal thing for a while until it wore itself out. That way my hopes would not get too high. Everyone hates disappointment and I have certainly had my share lately and didn't need any more. Off to bed.

Up and Adam the next morning after a restless night, I feel good. I made a friend at the non-profit and couldn't wait to tell him what had just happened to me. I am still a little dazed and confused but it was refreshing to hear anything positive from anyone in my life at this time. I was lifted by this letter to a level of forbearance which had not been there in a while. This came at the right time as the light in my tunnel was getting pretty dim. My friend asked me how I replied and I told him I hadn't yet. He asked me WHAT was I was waiting for. I told him I planned to email her that night after I got home from the restaurant as it was one of my nights to work. All day the brain churned up a variety of scenarios for my reply and wanted to make sure I used the proper tone when replying.

The restaurant was busy that night and I was bushed when I got home. I went straight to the computer and started an email reply to her letter. It sounded kind of generic as I had not heard from her in a while and didn't want to step on any toes. Hi, how have you been, what's new and I have been *great.* How about you? I really didn't want her to know where I was in life (pretty close to the bottom) as I didn't think it was really necessary. Remember I never planned on seeing her, it was just supposed to be a pen-pal thing. I told her some basic biography stuff, like the marriages and divorces, my children and where I was living. I gave her my emails addresses and phone numbers. I inquired about her life and told her to tell me everything in a synopsis as I had often thought about her through the years and I sometimes wondered whatever happened to her. After all it had been twenty-seven long years since I had spoken to her.

I must have redrafted this email five times before I was ready to send it. I finally said it was great to hear from you and we should stay in touch. I figured it was going to be something like facebook, when an old friend requests you to friend them and sends you a message. You friend them and reply and you have two or three communications until it dries up and you never speak again. After you get sick and tired of reading boring posts everyday about their senseless lives, it stops. Then you unfriend them. Now it is late in the morning and I have my exciting $10.00/hr job to go to in the morning, so I send the email.

I awaken after a few hours of sleep and got ready for work. I am not expecting a reply as it has only been a few hours since I sent the email, but curiosity got the best of me and I decided to check it anyway. Holy shit, a response!! It was a long response at that, and I didn't have time to read it, as I didn't want to be late for work. I didn't have a smart phone, so I couldn't read the email until later. I knew it was over two pages long and didn't want to punish myself by logging onto the company computer to read it so I waited until I got home. I hadn't been working there very long and my position was "nobody" so I decided it would be better to wait. I got home and took a shower and had some dinner. Getting ready to read this email was like getting ready for an important first date. I didn't want anything hanging over my head when I was ready to *consume* this reply.

She had a million questions and a million answers. I was glad she was doing well. She was working as a Registered Nurse at a Veterans Hospital and was making good money working third shift. She had three great kids and was no longer married. She had gone through two divorces and was not married currently. I told her as little as possible, avoiding the loser syndrome and the need to know concept, but she asked those types of questions anyway. It was a long email and I cherished every word as this is a woman I loved for a few years and I could tell in her email that the **something special** I once experienced was still there. Remember she always made me feel great. She ended her email on a high note and asked me to reply and I told her I would. Her late night shift explained why when she replied and the length of her replies as after three in the morning, all of her patients were tucked in and she had plenty of time to write lengthy emails. This was to become a tradition with her.

There was a lot of catching up to do. I let her know what has been going on in my life and her with me. There were years of history to discuss. There were my three failed marriages and her two. There were the kids to talk about, their dreams and accomplishments. So emails flew back and forth daily for a long time. She would send me one of her two pagers and I would religiously wake one hour early everyday to respond. It was a great start to my day. It didn't take long before I started to feel good about myself.

My financial situation hadn't changed but my spirit was definitely lifted. I was in a super mood all the time and was very happy to have her back in my life, even if the distance was great. Let's face it, I was plain old lonely. There was a lot of information that had been misplaced or forgotten over the time as we had not spoken, so there were a lot of questions. I discussed my second marriage to a woman who was a virgin. Sex was always a high priority in both our lives (Wendy's and mine) and life with my second wife wasn't cutting it in that department. I also revealed what happen to my third marriage in quite some detail. There were financial problems (gambling) caused by her, as well as numerous accusations of cheating until it just became unbearable. This became a huge issue I will discuss later. Wendy didn't seem to remember a lot of details about our lives together in New Jersey. She couldn't remember if we went out a lot or if we used to have sex a lot. I explained our lives as best as I could remember having sex like rabbits all the time and all the traveling we did to exotic places as my job would permit. I wondered why she hadn't remembered those precious moments and wondered if her cocaine use had any effect on that. She on the other had remembered some things I did not. For weeks we filled each other in on what had happened over our time then and the time in between. I am talking a lot of emails. It was probably between hers and mine, three pages a day for ninety days. Do the math that is 270 pages of just really good stuff.

The latter emails contained current feelings that had developed during this time period and desires and dreams for the future. This was starting to get serious? Or was it? It could just be that I am finally getting attention from anyone (doesn't really matter who). Loneliness will do that to you. That is why so many people get remarried to their rebound person so soon after divorcing.

14

There were daily emails back and forth as Wendy worked at night. Everyone but her hated that shift, so by three in the morning, all the patients were asleep. This was when she wrote her elongated emails. Throughout most days of the week we would swap some of the funnier stuff that floats around from mailbox to mailbox on the internet. I thought I would give you a little break and share some of our favorites. They made us smile or laugh back then and I am sure they will for you as well.

UNDER 30, YOU'VE GOT IT TOO EASY

When I was a kid, adults used to bore me to tears with their tedious diatribes about how hard things were. When they were growing up; what with walking Twenty-five miles to school every morning....

Uphill... barefoot...

BOTH ways

Yada, yada, yada

And I remember promising myself that when I grew up, there was no way in hell I was going to lay a bunch of crap like that on my kids about how hard I had it and how easy they've got it!

But now that... I'm over the ripe old age of thirty, I can't help but look around and notice the youth of today.

You've got it so easy! I mean, compared to my childhood, you live in a damn Utopia!
And I hate to say it, but you kids today, you don't know how good you've got it!

I mean, when I was a kid we didn't have The Internet. If we wanted to know something, we had to go to the damn library and look it up ourselves, in the card catalogue!!

There was no email!! We had to actually write somebody a letter - with a pen!

Then you had to walk all the way across the street and put it in the mailbox and it would take, like, a week to get there! Stamps were 10 cents!

Child Protective Services didn't care if our parents beat us. As a matter of fact, the parents of all my friends also had permission to kick our ass! Nowhere was safe!

There were no MP3's or Napsters! If you wanted to steal music, you had to hitchhike to the damn record store and shoplift it yourself!

Or you had to wait around all day to tape it off the radio and the DJ would usually talk over the beginning and @#% it all up! There were no CD players! We had tape decks in our car. We'd play our favorite tape and "eject" it when finished, and then the tape would come undone.*

We didn't have fancy crap like Call Waiting! If you were on the phone and somebody else called they got a busy signal, that's it! And we didn't have fancy Caller ID either! When the phone rang, you had no idea who it was! It could be your school, your mom, your boss, your bookie, your drug dealer, a collections agent, you just didn't know!!! You had to pick it up and take your chances, mister!

We didn't have any fancy Sony Playstation video games with high-resolution 3-D graphics! We had the Atari 2600! With games like 'Space Invaders' and 'Asteroids'. Your guy was a little square! You actually had to use your imagination!! And there were no multiple levels or screens; it was just one screen... forever!

And you could never win. The game just kept getting harder and harder and faster and faster until you died! Just like LIFE!

You had to use a little book called a TV Guide to find out what was on! You were screwed when it came to channel surfing! You had to get off your ass and walk over to the TV to change the channel! NO REMOTES!!!

There was no Cartoon Network either! You could only get cartoons on Saturday Morning. Do you hear what I'm saying!?! We had to wait ALL WEEK for cartoons, you spoiled little rat-bastards!

And we didn't have microwaves; if we wanted to heat something up we had to use the stove! Imagine that!

That's exactly what I'm talking about! You kids today have got it too easy. You're spoiled. You guys wouldn't have lasted five minutes back in 1980 or before!

Regards,
The Over 30 Crowd

7 DEGREES OF BLONDE

FIRST DEGREE

A married couple were asleep when the phone rang at 2 in the morning. The very blonde wife picked up the phone, listened a moment and said 'How should I know, that's 200 miles from here!' and hung up.

The husband said, 'Who was that?'

The wife answered, 'I don't know, some woman wanting to know if the coast is clear.'

SECOND DEGREE

Two blondes are walking down the street. One notices a compact on the sidewalk and leans down to pick it up. She opens it, looks in the mirror and says, 'Hmm, this person looks familiar.'

The second blonde says, 'Here, let me see!'

So, the first blonde hands her the compact.

The second blonde looks in the mirror and says, 'You dummy, it's me!'

THIRD DEGREE

A blonde suspects her boyfriend of cheating on her, so she goes out and buys a gun. She goes to his apartment unexpectedly and when she opens the door she finds him in the arms of a redhead. Well, the blonde is really angry. She opens her purse to take out the gun, and as she does so, she is overcome with grief. She takes the gun and puts it to her head.

The boyfriend yells, 'No, honey, don't do it!!!'

The blonde replies, 'Shut up, you're next!'

FOURTH DEGREE

A blonde was bragging about her knowledge of state capitals.

She proudly says, 'Go ahead, and ask me, I know 'em all. 'A friend says, 'OK, what's the capital of Wisconsin?'

The blonde replies, 'Oh, that's easy. It's W.'

FIFTH DEGREE

Q: What did the blonde ask her doctor when he told her she was pregnant?

A: 'Is it mine?'

SIXTH DEGREE

Bambi, a blonde in her fourth year as a UCLA Freshman, sat in her US Government class. The professor asked Bambi if she knew what Roe vs. Wade was about.

Bambi pondered the question; then, finally, said, 'That was the decision George Washington had to make before he crossed the Delaware.'

SEVENTH DEGREE

Returning home from work, a blonde was shocked to find her house ransacked and burglarized. She telephoned the police at once and reported the crime. The police dispatcher broadcast the call on the radio, and a K-9 unit, patrolling nearby, was the first to respond.

As the K-9 officer approached the house with his dog on a leash, the *blonde ran out on the porch, shuddered at the sight of the cop and his dog, then sat down on the steps. Putting her face in her hands, she moaned, 'I come home to find all my possessions stolen. I call the police for help, and what do they do? They send me a BLIND policeman!'*

THE BIKER

A man was riding his motorcycle along a California beach when suddenly the sky clouded above his head and, in a booming voice, the Lord said, "Because you have TRIED to be faithful to me in all ways, I will grant you one wish. The biker pulled over and said, "Build a bridge to Hawaii so I can ride over anytime I want."The Lord said, "Your request is materialistic, think of the enormous challenges for that kind of undertaking; the supports required to reach the bottom of the Pacific and the concrete and steel it would take! It will nearly exhaust several natural resources. I can do it, but it is hard for me to justify your desire for worldly things. Take a little more time and think of something that could possibly help mankind.

The biker thought about it for a long time. Finally, he said, "Lord, I wish that I and all men could understand women; I want to know how she feels inside, what she's thinking when she gives me the silent treatment, why she cries, what she means when she says nothing's wrong, and how I can make a woman truly happy."
The Lord replied: "Do you want two lanes or four on that bridge?"

GIRLS NIGHT OUT

Two women friends had gone for a girl's night out. Both were very faithful and loving wives; however they had gotten over-enthusiastic on the Bacardi Breezers.
Incredibly drunk and walking home they needed to pee, so they stopped in the cemetery. One of them had nothing to wipe with so she thought she would take off her panties and use them. Her friend however was

wearing a rather expensive pair of panties
and did not want to ruin them.

She was lucky enough to squat down next to a grave that had a wreath with a ribbon on it, so she proceeded to wipe with that. After the girls did their business they proceeded to go home.
The next day one of the woman's husband was concerned that his normally sweet and innocent wife was still in bed hung over, so he phoned the other husband and said:

'These girls nights have got to stop! I'm starting to suspect the worst. My wife came home with no panties!!'
'That's nothing' said the other husband,
'Mine came back with a card stuck to her ass that said.....

'From all of us at the Fire Station. We'll never forget you."

CUSTOMER SERVICE

It happened at the Denver Airport. This is hilarious. I wish I had the guts of this girl. For all of you out there who've had to deal with an irate customer, this one is for you. An award should go to the United Airlines
Gate agent in Denver for being smart and funny, while making her point.

When confronted with a passenger who probably deserved to fly as cargo.
A crowded United Airlines flight was canceled. A single agent was
Re-booking a long line of inconvenienced travelers. Suddenly an angry passenger
pushed his way to the desk. He slapped his ticket on the counter and said,
"I HAVE to be on this flight and it has to be FIRST CLASS."

The agent replied, "I am sorry, sir. I'll be happy to try to help you, but I've got to help these folks first, and

*I'm sure we'll be able to work
something out."
The passenger was unimpressed.
He asked loudly, so that the
passengers
behind him could hear, "DO YOU
HAVE ANY IDEA WHO I AM?"
Without hesitating, the agent smiled
and grabbed her Public Address
Microphone, "May I have your
attention please, "She began, her
voice heard
clearly throughout the terminal."We
have a passenger here at Gate 14
WHO
DOES NOT KNOW WHO HE IS.
If anyone can help him find his
identity, please
come to Gate 14."
With the folks behind him in line
laughing hysterically, the man
glared at
The United agent, gritted his teeth
and swore "F*** You!"
Without flinching, she smiled and
said, I'm sorry sir, you'll have to get
In Line for that too."*

THE 11TH HUSBAND!!!

A young man married a beautiful woman who had previously divorced 10 husbands. On their wedding night, she told her new husband to "Please be gentle; I'm still a virgin."

"What?" said the puzzled groom? "How can that be if you've been married ten times?"

Well husband #1 was a Sales Rep; he kept telling me how great it was going to be.

Husband #2 was in Software Services; he was never really sure how it was supposed to function; but he said he'd look into it and get back to me.

Husband #3 was from Field Services; he said that everything checked out diagnostically but he just couldn't get the system up.

Husband#4 was in telemarketing; even though he knew he had the order, he didn't know when he would be able to deliver.

Husband #5 was an Engineer; he

understood the basic process but he wanted three years to research, implement and design a new state-of-the-art method.

Husband #6 was from Administration; he thought he knew how but he wasn't sure whether it was his job or not.

Husband #7 was in Marketing; although he had a product, he was never sure how to position it.

Husband #8 was a Psychiatrist; all he did was talk about it.

Husband #9 was a Gynecologist; all he did was look at it.

Husband #10 was a Stamp Collector;
all he ever did was _ _ _ _ _ _. God I miss him!!

But now that I've married you, I'm so excited.

"Wonderful" said the husband, but why?"

You're with the GOVERMENT.

141

This time <u>I KNOW</u> I'M gonna get
<u>*SCREWED!!*</u>

FALL CLASSES FOR WOMEN

At

THE ADULT LEARNING CENTER

REGISTRATION MUST BE
COMPLETED
By Monday, November 9, 2009

NOTE: DUE TO THEIR
COMPLEXITY AND
DIFFICULTLEVEL, CLASS SIZE
WILL BE LIMITED TO 8
PARTICIPANTS MAXIMUM.

Class 1

Up in Winter, Down in Summer -
How to Adjust a Thermostat, Step
by Step,

<u>*Slide Presentation*</u>.

Meets 4 wks, Monday
and Wednesday for 2

hrs, beginning at 7:00 PM.

Class 2

Which Takes More Energy - Putting the Toilet Seat Down, or Bitching About It for 3 Hours?

<u>*Round Table Discussion.*</u>
Meets 2 weeks, Saturday 12:00PM for 2 hours.

Class 3
Is It Possible To Drive Past a Wal-Mart Without Stopping?
<u>*Group Debate*</u>*.*
Meets 4 weeks, Saturday 10:00 AM for 2 hours.

Class 4

Fundamental Differences between a Purse and a Suitcase

<u>*Pictures and Explanatory Graphics*</u>*.*

Meets Saturdays at
2:00 PM for 3 weeks.

Class 5
Curling Irons--Can They Levitate
and Fly into the Bathroom Cabinet?
Examples on Video.
Meets 4 weeks, Tuesday and
Thursday for 2 hours beginning at
7:00 PM

Class 6
How to Ask Questions during
Commercials and Be Quiet during
the Program
Help Line Support and Support
Groups.
Meets 4 Weeks, Friday and Sunday
7:00 PM

Class 7
Can a Bath Be Taken Without 14
Different Kinds of Soaps and
Shampoos?
Open Forum.
Monday at 8:00 PM, 2 hours.

Class 8
Health Watch -- They Make
Medicine for PMS - USE IT!

Three nights; Monday, Wednesday, Friday at 7:00 PM for 2 hours.

Class 9
I Was Wrong and He Was Right
Real Life Testimonials!
Tuesdays at 6:00 PM Location to be determined.

Class 10
How to Parallel Park in Less Than 20 Minutes without an Insurance Claim.
Driving Simulations.
4 weeks, Saturday's noon, 2 hours.

Class 11

Learning to Live--How to Apply Brakes without Throwing Passengers through the Windshield.

Tuesdays at 7:00 PM, location to be determined

145

Class 12

How to Shop by Yourself.

Meets 4wks, Tuesday and Thursday for 2 hours beginning at 7:00 PM.

Upon completion of any of the above courses, diplomas will be issued to the survivors.

****

10 Reasons why Trick or Treating is Better than Sex!

> 10- You are guaranteed a little something in the sack.
>
> 9- If you get tired you can wait 10 minutes, then go at it again.
>
> 8- The uglier you look, the easier it is to get some.
>
> 7- You don't have to compliment

the person who gave you some.
>
> 6- It's ok when the person fantasies that you are someone else, cause you are!

> 5- Twenty years from now you'll still like candy.
                              >
> 4- If you don't like what you get, you can always go next door.

> 3- It doesn't matter if your kids hear you moaning and groaning.

> 2- Less guilt the morning after.

> And the number one reason why Trick or Treating is better than sex...
> You can do the whole neighborhood!

WHY DO CONDOMS COME IN BOXES OF 3, 6, AND 12???

A man walks into a drug store with his 8-year old son. They happen to walk by the condom display, and the boy asks, "What are these, Dad?"

To which the man matter-of-factly replies, "Those are called condoms, son. Men use them to have safe sex."

"Oh, I see," replied the boy pensively. "I've heard of that in health class at school." He looks over the display and picks up a package of 3 and asks, "Why are there 3 in this package?"

The dad replies, "Those are for high school boys, one for Friday, one for Saturday, and one for Sunday."

"Cool" says the boy. He notices a 6 pack and asks, "Then, who are these for?"

"Those are for college men," the dad answers. "TWO for Friday, TWO for Saturday, and TWO for

Sunday."

"WOW!" exclaimed the boy, "Then, who uses THESE?" he asks, picking up a 12-pack.
With a sigh and a tear in his eye, the dad replied, "Those are for married men. One for January, one for February, one for March......."

A ROMANTIC NOVEL

He grasped me firmly, but gently, just above my elbow and guided me into a room, his room.
Then he quietly shut the door and we were alone.
He approached me soundlessly, from behind, and spoke in a low, reassuring voice, close to my ear.
"Just relax. . . "
Without warning, he reached down and I felt his strong, calloused hands start at my ankles, gently probing and moving upward along

*my calves, slowly, but steadily. My
breath caught in my throat. I knew I
should be afraid, but somehow I
didn't care. His touch was so
experienced, so sure.*

*When his hands moved up onto my
thighs, I gave a slight shudder, and I
partly closed my eyes. My pulse
was pounding. I felt his knowing
fingers caress my abdomen, my
ribcage. And then, as he cupped my
firm, full breasts in his hands, I
inhaled sharply.*

*Probing, searching, knowing what
he wanted, he brought his hands to
my shoulders, slid them down my
tingling spine and into my panties.
Although I knew nothing about this
man, I felt oddly trusting and
expectant. This is a man, I thought.
A man used to taking charge. A man
not used to taking "no" for an
answer. A man who would tell me
what he wanted. A man who would
look into my soul and say . . . . .*

*"Okay, ma'am, you can board your
flight now.*

SMART KID

For his birthday, little Joe asked for a 10-speed bicycle. His father said, "Son, we'd give you one, but the mortgage on this house is $280,000 & your mother just lost her job. There's no way we can afford it." The next day the father saw little Joe heading out the front door with a suitcase. So he asked, "Son, where are you going?" Little Joe told him; "I was walking past your room last night and heard you telling mom you were pulling out. Then I heard her tell you to wait because she was coming too. And I'll be damned if I'm staying here by myself with a $280,000 mortgage & no bike."

I hope you enjoyed your little break. It's healthy to laugh as well as to cry.

Emails were not only for each other's entertainment. There were problems which came from them. Wendy and I were always honest with each other as it is still the best policy. One day my son and I had a huge fight about me disrespecting his Mom. He read my emails!! I tried

151

to explain to Wendy what happened to this marriage. She asked and she needed to know. I gave the best explanation I knew how to. I was accused of having affairs on repeated occasions; she had a gambling problem which created a financial burden on the family and just a whole bunch of me pouring my heart out. One night while my son was on a visitation day, I had to run to the grocery store. At this point he is fifteen and is not going to understand anything he is about to read. I left my email box opened and minimized it and went to the store. It was a private company email address, so it was not like he went onto Google or Yahoo and stumbled across it. It was minimized in the lower tray and he opened it out of curiosity? That is invasion of privacy, but this was my son. I felt betrayed. He rarely understood my side of the divorce story and sided with his Mom. It was at the tender stages of the divorce and kids are just plain old mad that it's not working out between their parents. The bigger problem was he didn't stop after reading one. He continued to open and read more. Some of these emails contained information that was rated "R" and he was not only, not old enough to read them, but there was some pretty adult stuff in them about Wendy's and my past that should have only been read by us. My son and I fought for a day and a half and were hardly speaking after it was over, as he was hurt. The truth usually does. My ex-wife gambled away over our fifteen years together, over one hundred thousand dollars. That my friend is a financial strain.

Wendy sensed something was wrong and inquired as to what was up and I told her. She was furious! She also felt betrayed and hurt and really let me have it for leaving my email open. She was right. I closed it after that everytime but it was too late. Wendy freaked out as she was upset enough to end the whole relationship. She used phrases like, this was a mistake, maybe we should end this now, maybe we should never talk again, and how can I ever meet your son. She really wanted to meet my son, as I believe that someday she wanted to get back together with me permanently.

This was a crossroad I was not sure how to handle.

As trying not to think about it as we communicated daily, I tried to explain that this issue should not get in the way of our future. I was pleading for her to listen to me now. Wendy always had to have things her way. She was always stubborn and had to do things on her terms. She consulted with Karen her best friend since middle school and I think she had a great deal to do with her finally realizing that she should accept it and shrug it off. She agreed to let it go and it was never spoken of again. The communication continued as the emails and phone calls still happened but it wasn't going any further than that. I was happy just having someone in my life. Wendy had always been "the one that got away". She made me feel, always, the best one person could make another person feel. She was simply amazing to me.

15

She fired a tomahawk at me with her next email saying she was coming to visit. It didn't say I was thinking of coming to visit you for the weekend, what do you think or what is your schedule? It said I booked a flight and will be there in three weeks. Wow! My first reaction was I was pissed! I hate when people control my life. I told her that the next time we spoke on the phone. She didn't confer with me. She just went and did it. Was this a problem? It was now as I had to fess up about my loser life.

There goes Wendy always doing things on her terms. She was physically going to be here and soon. Wendy, now forcing me to change gears about all the truth, changed my approach about our future communication. It's like saying I was between careers, not I was in a rut. I used to be a highly respected individual in corporate life and in the social community. Now I am in a hibernation mode, laying low for a while. I need to tell her because she needs to know. If she is the person I think she is, she will help me. As her arrival date approached, she asked questions like do you have a camera, what is the dress code for dinner; do you own a pair of flip-flops?

I finally came clean and told her how broke I was and I didn't own a camera, flip-flops, and didn't own a pair of sneakers or jeans. This was painful but honesty is always the best policy, always. You roll the dice and see who your true friends are. That's the way it goes. Its better that way, trust me. She understood, as she knew me. She finally remembered all the good things I did for her and what kind of person I was when we were together. After the anger of not consulting me about her trip wore off, excitement began to grow inside me day by day.

I was about to see that vibrant smile that I have not seen in so many years. I would get a warm hug and be able to touch her warm heart once again. I would be in her caring arms and see her in every amazing way I remembered her.

My moods were great and I had to ask all my bosses for time off. I was like a little kid playing baseball hitting his first home run. I told everyone what was going on. Everyone knew I needed some positive change in my life and this would be it. My non-profit boss approved my time off and my part time job was just a matter of switching one day. She was to arrive on a Monday which was a visitation day for my son. At his age of 15 years old now, he had lots of social obligations, school, martial arts, and friends, that he blew me off more times than I can remember on days I was supposed to see him. I figured this would not be a problem if I switch one day with him. I told him, a friend from out of town was coming to visit for a few days and I would not be able to see him on Monday. I told him to tell his Mom and I would make it up to him that weekend. This didn't go so well as after discovering that he was secretly reading my emails, which I did not password protect, my bad, he was pissed. He was especially concerned about the email to Wendy that explained what happened to the marriage between his Mom and me. There was a little bashing going on because at this point he thought I was to blame for the whole divorce. He thought his Mom was a poor victim of my inconsiderate and impassionate behavior. So I struggled with this for a few weeks and thought everything was settled. This was not so. When I dropped him off on Sunday I reminded him of the upcoming days and I would not be seeing him on Monday. He not only forgot himself, he forgot to tell his Mom. My ex-wife was still in the early divorce stages where the husband needs to follow the visitation rules to the letter. They were both furious. Of course she forgot about all the times that he blew me off. That is how it gets during a divorce, beyond ugly.

Excitement continued to build as we continued to talk everyday as well as the lengthy emails. The arrival of Wendy got closer and something inside me started to change. There was a positive attitude that I have not seen in a while in me. I started to plan everything for her arrival. I scrubbed my house from top to bottom and planned a reception at the airport that included a rose just for her. The rose idea was based on one of my favorite songs by Kenny Rogers, entitled "Buy Me a Rose".

"Buy me a rose, Call me from work,
Open a door for me what would it hurt,
Tell me you love me
with the look in your eyes,
These are the little things,
I need the most in my life".

I even went out and bought the CD, so I could play it on the way home from the airport. Then the day came.

I was nervous as the pics she sent me were not as I remembered her and I was actually fearful that I would not recognize her at the airport, how stupid. Of course, I show up early in case her plane caught a tail wind and arrived early. Watching the reader board at the airport her plane had landed and now the tension was building. I ask the information attendant about her flight and she noticed the rose and she said "someone's a lucky woman".

Watching the deplaning passengers, I immediately recognized her as she looked like she hadn't changed at all. Remember it has been 27 years. She looked just like I remembered her. She was wearing heals, a black and white sundress with spaghetti straps, and was also wearing a great tan. She had a better tan than I did and I live in Florida. The only thing I didn't recognize was her breast. She was pretty much flat chested when we dated. Now she was proudly displaying a gorgeous set of full C's. They looked amazing. Her first husband was a plastic surgeon. WOW, what a look! She was beautiful. We approached each other and at this point I still don't know how this is going to feel. Honestly, I was nervous. We embrace, kissed and said Hi! At this point, you could have hit me with a baseball bat and I am certain that I wouldn't have felt it. I gave her the rose. This was amazing.

 We went to baggage claim, holding hands on the way to get her bags and headed off to my car to go HOME. Home is a strange word, as it has different meanings for different people in different situations. I am past excited, loaded the CD as she tried to molest me in the car and I stopped her. My driving record was not the greatest after my DUI and I was scared to death of cops. I asked her to wait until we got home and she agreed. Arriving home, we unpacked her stuff into the house and into my son's room as he was not going to be around for a few days. That was when the sexual reunion started. I was nervous as I hadn't had sex in over three years. I hoped it was like riding a bike. Immediately into the bedroom and no stopping for almost an hour. Fantastic does not do justice to the way this was going for me. We held each other after sex for several minutes which felt like hours. Unless you have experienced something like this before, you have no idea what I was feeling. If you have been in a situation like this before, you know exactly how I was feeling. It has been twenty-seven years!

A little unpacking was going on as well as some small conversation. Remember we had been talking for hours in the months past as well as all the emails. I almost thought we were talked out. That turned out not to be true. True love is when you never have to say anything and I was feeling that now. I planned a trip to our famous number one rated beach in the world to witness the sunset. I had prepared a Roasted Pork Loin dinner with Oven Roasted Potatoes and Carrots. I set-up dinner, turned the oven on and we were off to the beach. It was a short drive, 20 minutes, and not realizing that Wendy lived in the mid-west, a beach sunset was a huge deal. We sat and watch the sunset and then we went for a walk. Hand in hand we walked for a quite a while. It felt like we were never apart. I mean never. It all came back and the only word I can use to describe the whole weekend is comfortable. There was nothing that needed to be talk about, there were no dating issues as there is with dating, there was just us. We headed home and had a great dinner. Wendy usually ate out or ordered out so she appreciated a good home cooked meal. The reunion was now as real as it gets.

After dinner she only had one thing on her mind, sex. I knew she had some recent relationships in the past but I guess masturbating in the Tanning Salon wasn't cutting it or any of those relationships either. Let me paint you a picture. A gorgeous woman, perfect c-cups breast, flat stomach, nicely tanned, masturbating stark naked in a tanning booth. Got it? She knew her body very well, every square inch. It had been three years for me. Yeah, you're reading that right. Three years since my ex-wife and I did it and I was not interested in getting involved with anyone else. So I refrained. I was also ready. Three years is a very long for someone who liked sex as much as I did. There was the task of walking the dogs left on the list of things to do that night and I told her I would be back in twenty minutes. To my surprise, she insisted on coming with me. I was impressed, so I let her come with me and we did the mile around the block. This has always told me something about her. She cared completely about me including everything in my life like my dogs. We started the walk and she grabbed a leash from me for one of the dogs and she took temporary ownership. She never stopped impressing me. The comfort setting is set on max as I am not sure I have felt this way since the last time we were together. We had experienced a lot of walks on many beaches over the years. We arrived home and got ready for our first night back together again. As I stared into her eyes, I saw happiness. Have you ever really looked into someone eyes? I don't mean looked at, I mean looked into. Happiness was now in my eyes as well.

 So off to the bedroom we go again. She is not into foreplay as I remember. She just wants to get to it. I offer to take some Viagra as I am not a spring chicken anymore and Wendy tells me I won't need it. We engage in sex and it literally feels like no time has passed in the last twenty-seven years. The only difference is that she now knew her body better than she did before and communication between each other was never a problem. We always talked to each other in bed. There were some side positions and then I was on top and hitting the G-Spot with all cylinders. Orgasms started to happen for her and a little moaning and screaming as I guess she learned a little about expressing herself in the bedroom over the last few decades. After four or five orgasms I asked her to get on top. It was my favorite grand finale position. She got up on the balls of her feet and just rode me to a fantastic orgasm.

We rolled over and kissed for a while and little needed to be said. We assumed the spoon position and sailed off to sleep in minutes, both feeling the same. It was like we were never apart. The comfort level was off the charts. I haven't slept that good in over three years. Totally relaxed we slept for eight hours without incident. Even the dogs didn't wake me for their usual bathroom break at two in the morning. She had been burning the candle at both ends for a few days, working at the hospital and tending bar at the park and I knew she was tired. I was just this side of heaven. That's why I slept so well. Morning came as there was no alarm clock to set and I had a full day planned. I made coffee and it was a great morning, I made some breakfast, home fries, omelets and pastries. We ate and chatted. Now she brought out some presents that she had bought me. This woman had a heart of gold. Everyone knew that. She bought me Flip-flops as I didn't have a pair and she knew we were going to the beach today. She also bought me a Digital Camera as she also knew I didn't have one. This was so we could record the events of this weekend. She bought the camera at the PX, as there was a store for the Veterans in the lobby of the hospital. She also bought me some cologne, Burberry. I had never heard of it and in my financial position, I refrained from buying non essential items. I considered this a non-essential as I didn't date. It smelled great. We had another cup of coffee and Wendy wanted to check her email. I set her up on my computer. This feeling could only be described as easy, as she was wearing only a t-shirt and sipping coffee in my home. This was great. Next on the list was sex before a shower. I didn't argue as I told you, I love sex. We went back to the bedroom and now it was a little different. There was a lot more caressing, touching, kissing of various body parts and more intensity in general. This session was better than the last one.

The first stop was the restaurant that I worked at as she wanted to see where I worked. She showered and dressed and ask me a strange question, I thought. Hat or no hat? She was holding a baseball cap and asked me my opinion about whether to wear it or not. I said hat and we were on our way. She looked great as she was wearing a swimsuit under her shorts and t-shirt, but I just couldn't get over those perfect C-Cups. They looked awesome. We arrived and sat down and Yvette waited on us and introduced herself. Everyone I cared about knew she was coming to town and Yvette was on that list so she knew who she was. I introduced her to Wendy. We ate and talked and enjoyed the first part of the morning. My boss stopped by the table to say hello and asked "what is a beautiful woman like her doing with a guy like me?"He picked up the check and I left a ten dollar tip. It was the least I could do. At this point it's only ten in the morning and a lot has happened so far. Wendy is only going to be here for 76 hours so I wanted every one of them to count. We headed to the beach.

16

The beach was beautiful. There was three hundred feet of white sugary sand between us and the water. The water was crystal clear and it was about eighty degrees. It was perfect. It is no wonder why this beach is rated number one in the world year after year. We stripped down to our swimsuits and applied lotion and she looked great. She had a great tan as she went to a tanning salon regularly and I had a farmers tan as I worked outside and wore a t-shirt and never went to the beach. On the other hand, I didn't look so great. She noticed I was thin, lost weight, and hadn't worked out in some time. As I look back at the photos taken that day, with my new camera, I could see how right she was. She still loved me anyway. We went for a swim which she really enjoyed as she had never been to this beach and hadn't been to the Gulf of Mexico since she had last seen her Dad some years ago. He didn't live far from me. We were embraced in each other's arms, facing each other and just floating, weightlessly without a care in the world. After the swim we went for a long walk. Walking hand in hand, that comfort feeling continued as I was still feeling that time had not passed. That **_something special_** about her and how she made me feel has endured all these years. Simply unbelievable!

The conversation was casual and limited. There was no need to talk, no need to impress and nothing to prove. We still knew each other inside and out. After a few hours at the beach we decided to return home to nap as Wendy was still exhausted from working the night shift the night before leaving. She had no sleep as she got home from work, packed and got ready to go to the airport to see her old boyfriend. She had also worked Friday, Saturday and Sunday at the water park, bartending. I knew she was exhausted. She had been running on pure adrenaline for four days now. I guess she was just as excited to see me, as I was to see her.

After arriving home you can probably guess what was on her

mind to do next. She had a surprise for me as we showered and she put on one of my t-shirts. She asked me to lie on my huge couch and become naked. I obeyed as she began what turned out to be the longest blowjob of my life. She began by sucking on my toes which raise an interesting tidbit in our former relationship. One of her favorite sayings was "Suck on my Toes and I'll take off my Clothes". It reminded me of the song "Bubbly" by Colbie Caillat.

"Starts in my toes, makes me crinkle my nose…. Where ever you go, I'll always know…. cause you make me smile here wherever you go"

I told her that whenever I heard that song, it reminded me of her. She was extremely surprised to hear that I thought about her and asked why I never tried to contact her. Over the years, when I was in St. Louis, I never tried to contact her because I do not live in the past. I believed that I would never see her again. While I was in St. Louis I was married to my second wife and happy. There was no desire to look her up. She understood.

Back to the best blowjob ever. The best part about performing oral sex on someone is not only the skill involved, it's the non-selfish effort that is put into it. Wendy was totally committed to her effort. This blowjob included a prostate massage as well, which intensified my eventual orgasm. It took a total of about forty-five minutes which I think is longer than any porn film as they just use it as an appetizer for intercourse. This was the appetizer, entrée and dessert all in one. Wendy asked if I had anything that I had to do as she really wanted to take a nap.
.

I told her I had some emails to read and some phone calls to make so I told her to go ahead. I really didn't have to do any of those things, but I thought she would feel better if she thought I did. She quickly fell asleep on the couch. She looked so peaceful and beautiful as she lay there. Because she was asleep, she couldn't see me pinching myself to see if this was really happening. I was really surprised that after fifteen hours, there were no issues about how I felt. The nervousness was gone and I felt totally stupendous. I let her sleep as we had a big evening planned later on.

We had planned to go to a trendy tourist restaurant on the beach. The food was average at best, but the atmosphere was awesome. I told her I was buying dinner as my way of thanking her for coming down. She wouldn't hear of it. She insisted on paying for dinner. I didn't argue with her as I knew her only too well. Arguing with her was just a waste of energy. Another shower is in order as we dress casual for dinner. She insisted on buying dinner as, after being honest with her, she now knew how bleak my financial situation was. Everyone in Florida dresses casual unless you are going to the theater or the Ritz. We were not.

We arrive and got seated on the deck. We could see the street of this beach village. The restaurant is located on the beach but it is not a waterfront restaurant. People go there for the atmosphere of the village and to watch the people and enjoy whatever entertainment is happening. In other words, the restaurant faces the street not the Gulf. Wendy orders a Virgin Pina Colada as she has been clean and sober for years now. She has come back in fantastic form from a life of addiction and is one of the most positive people I know. Her glass is always half full, not half empty. All her text messages end with the automated phrase "Life is Good". I ordered a beer, as I have not seen the light yet of the benefits not to drink. We order dinner. Wendy orders straight off the menu and I have to create my own dish. I knew they had scallops on the menu because it was a combo dish served with shrimp. I love Scallops and wanted to get just Scallops. The waitress said that it was ok. I decided to push it a little more as I wanted to change the preparation. I used to be a Chef so I know by looking at the ingredients on the menu, what is actually available. As long as there is a real Chef in the kitchen, anything is possible. However, there is danger in ordering something that is not on the menu. If you order an item that is prepared thousands of times, the odds of it coming out right are very good. If you order some special, like I just did, and there is some unqualified cook in charge that night, the odds are not good that this will be the meal of a lifetime. Just remember that little piece of advice.

Dinner arrives and is consumed. We started with Oysters, then salads and then the entrees. As I said the food is average at best and it was this time too. Wendy had Shrimp and enjoyed it and I had my special meal which was okay. I deserved what I got though. Enjoying each other's company and the ambience of the atmosphere, we ask the waitress to take some pictures of us and she agrees. She asked what the occasion was, if it was a birthday, anniversary or what. We explained to her that we used to date twenty-seven years ago and this was our first reunion. She was amazed by our story and thought that it unique as she was not even born when Wendy and I first started dating. She obliged and took several pictures which to this day I cherish. They came out great. Wendy looked greater than ever and I had this huge smile stuck on my face, which even I hadn't seen in some time. As I look back at these pictures, I wish I had an older photo of her to compare it to. She looked so much like she did decades ago. The years had treated her well. She had beautiful brown hair, shoulder length, pretty brown eyes, a gorgeous smile and a face that was so familiar and radiant. She actually looked better than she did the first time I dated her. Can you tell I was in love with this woman all over again? I've been in love many times, so I don't have to get hit by a bus to recognize it. Of course, love is dangerous and I wasn't worried about it this time, as nothing has ever felt this good.

After dinner we walked the village and stopped to buy some t-shirts for her kids. We headed home. We made the twenty minute drive home and held hands most of the way. Not many words were spoken, but they didn't need to. I felt that I had been in love for fifty years to the only woman God created for me. We were definitely soul mates. This is how I felt. I found out much later from Wendy's best friend since middle school, that she felt exactly the same way too on this reunion trip. Thus far, I realize that I am in the middle of the best three days I have ever had in my entire life.

We get home and you guessed it. There is only one thing to do before retiring for the night. More sex! I am not sure anyone is counting the number of times we did it, but Wendy claims it was ten times in seventy-six hours. She must have taken advantage of me when I was sleeping, as I can only remember seven! I couldn't wait to make love to her again. Making love is different than having sex. Sex is a physical activity by itself. Having sex with someone you are totally in love with and are completely connected with is a whole lot bigger experience. It's the touch, the little things; the nothing about her bothers me "effect", which generates that feeling of total love. We were there. Love making was great and lasted a good hour as Wendy always had several orgasms during our love making session and I was lucky to have two. We made love until we both fell asleep for the night. Again it was the most restful night of sleep for another night. Right about now I feel twenty years younger.

Morning has arrived and it's Wendy last day with me before she has to return home. I review our agenda of the things we wanted to do while she was here and it's pretty much complete. I woke her while she was sleeping with a little cunnilingus action of my own and we made love to start the day out right. Everyday should either start or end that way. Both, if you have the time in your regular daily lives. However we know this was a special occasion. Wendy's plane leaves at five in the evening and I have to be back at work at four. I made breakfast as she loved my cooking, had coffee, checked emails and then showered to go out. Wendy wanted to do some shopping and I was going to squeeze some errands in. My Mom was sick and in the hospital and I had some banking to do. We were gone most of the morning and we talked about our reunion and life in general. She asked a strange question of me this time. She asked me how many times a day I thought would we make love. I asked her to clarify. After she goes home tonight, none. She explained if we were together, what I thought the number of times per week we would make love. I found out years later what she meant by that. I am still convinced that we eventually going to be together forever. We have to.

After running around all day, we returned home about lunchtime. Wendy dragged me into the bedroom for what she called, one last time before she goes. Who am I to argue? I hadn't had any in three years. I had a lot of catching up to do. I knew this would be the last time for a while. I would have to save up money to visit her next, as it would be my turn. So I knew we better make this count. We both gave this session a little extra effort. There was so much excitement in the air for the last three days. It was hard to comprehend. During this final effort Wendy began to moan which turned into screaming as multiple orgasms followed in succession. She was actually quite loud. I asked her to lower the volume as someone may call the police in fear that someone was getting killed or being hurt. She laughed and continued to enjoy our last hurrah.

Famished after that, Wendy wanted to know if there was a Firehouse restaurant in my neighborhood, as it was her favorite sub shop. I explained that there was one right down the street and I asked what she wanted. Corned Beef was an excellent choice as they make great hot sandwiches. I told her I would be right back and left to go get the food. I picked up the food and upon my return home, my heart sank in my chest with a terrible feeling. As you make the turn down my street, there is a straight view of my house for almost three blocks. I could see EMS, with lights flashing, parked outside my house. I thought to myself, someone called the police because of the noise generated during our last session. This should prove to be interesting. I wonder how they are going to write this one up. Wendy was as healthy as an Ox and I knew she wasn't having a heart attack so there was no other explanation. I hope to God, I didn't kill her with my passion. As I got closer, all kinds of shit was racing through my mind, I now realized that the EMS unit was parked one house down, not in front of my house. It was my neighbors Dad who was taken away for some medical reason that I never found out why. I was relieved and as it turned out, it is now just a funny story. We had lunch and laughed all throughout the meal. This is definitely a story that will never be forgotten.

I washed some clothes for her as she began to pack for her trip home. Now I am finally realizing that she is leaving and became sad. This was the greatest weekend of my life and I just never wanted it to end. I kept thinking I didn't know what to expect after this. We were both feeling the same thing but it was better for both of us not to say anything. There would be nothing but crying and consoling and making promises that we might not be able to keep.

The hour finally came as I got ready for work and drove her to the airport. She checked in and I walked her to her gate. The funny feeling in my gut said several things to me. It asked the questions like, would I ever see her again or is this, the start of something that would last a lifetime or something in-between? Her plane wasn't departing for a while and she had plenty of time but she asked me to leave so I would not be late for work. She always had good ethics. I really didn't want to leave but she was right. She was usually right and it was always senseless to argue with her. She was very intelligent. Now it was time to say good-bye which I didn't want to do either but I had to. A warm long embrace which included a well connected kiss happened and I began to cry. Was this happiness or sadness. You decide. I think it was both. She told me to "stop". I left the airport in tears and imbedded her visit in my mind forever. I drove to work and could not focus on anything but her. I would miss her smile and her energy that she radiated wherever she went. Upon my arrival everyone asked how her visit went. I told them it was fantastic and held my composure. Everyone could see by the glow on my face that I was the happiest man in the world. The night was busy and that was a good thing as it took my mind off my Wendy. After work, I arrived home and began to digest what had just conspired. That ***something special*** that she once had was still there and always would be. People used to ask me if I would ever marry again. I always answered quickly, no. That was before her visit. If there was ever woman for me it was Wendy and YES I would marry her and it would be forever. She was the ***one***.

I asked her to text me when she landed and she did. The next morning there was an extended email thanking me for my hospitality as she was always proper and polite. Now the question is what happens next?

17

So what does happen now? We continued to talk almost daily and the long emails continued to flow as well. After her visit something came over me. We made a promise. I told her I would gain fifteen pounds by the next time I saw her and she promised to lose ten pounds, although I didn't think she needed to. You know women think they can never be too thin. It was like watching the movie "Rocky III". It was the inspiration that Sylvester Stallone got when he is determined to kick Clubber Lang's ass. Wendy had given my life purpose and a really great reason to live. I decided to start to work out and we both agreed I needed to gain some weight back. I had lost fifteen pounds during my divorce process. I was going to get it back. My daily work-out consisted of a series of calisthenics including push-ups, crunches and stretching exercises. It also included weight lifting. I did military presses, curls, reverse curls, and bicep curls. I stretched every day, the back, the hamstrings and the neck. I worked out almost every day as I was motivated to gain the weight that I promised Wendy I would. After six weeks or so I started to look a whole lot better. I ate three square meals a day sometimes even more. I had orange and cranberry juice every morning as well as taking Vitamin C in large doses. Every few days I increased the number of reps and the amount of weight to increase my muscle mass resulting in weight gain. I started to drink supplement drinks to add weight as well. At this point in my life, my attitude now was I wanted to live forever.

I discovered Apricot Kernels. In a study performed in the 1970's, cancer patients were given high doses of vitamin B-17 for treatment. B-17 can be found in fruits like strawberries and yes, apricot kernels. After several months of treatment, these patients, in most cases had no signs of cancer. It was gone. There were no more tumors and no more symptoms. The experiment was buried by the government as if there was a natural cure for cancer available, the pharmaceutical business would be greatly affected. I read this online somewhere after a friend on Facebook turned me onto the idea. I researched a little further and figured that since I was a former smoker of thirty years and both of my parents died of cancer, I would give it a try. I found a source for them at a site called Apricot Power.com. They were not at all expensive, as they are the kernels that most apricot manufacturers discard. I ordered them and they arrived. After reading the instructions and warnings I started to take them as part of my daily ritual. Be careful if you start taking them. The research says that the dosage was six to seven kernels per day. Trust me, start with one a day and every other day increase your dosage until you get to the six or seven per day. If you don't, you will experience severe headaches and dizziness. Good things take time. In a matter of twelve weeks time I had gain ten pounds. The goal was fifteen. I couldn't seem to go beyond that weight as I have an ectoskeletal build. I am skinny by nature. I continued to work out and continued to look pretty impressive. I was happy with myself and couldn't wait to show Wendy on my visit to her place, as it would be my turn to travel. God, I felt good. I became more positive and aggressive at work, in a good way. Everyone I worked with noticed the change. My co-worker, at the restaurant, Yvette took me aside one day and told me that I used to be a little bit of an asshole and appeared to be a "Grumpy Old Man" at work. But she said, lately there has been an amazing and significantly noticeable change. Most of my co-workers asked about her and us daily. It was what I considered normal to be in a relationship and to love and to be loved. It was fantastic.

After Wendy went home I went to visit my Mom who was in the hospital. She was ill suffering from many things. She had blood clots in her legs, had colon cancer and a host of other problems. She was eighty years old and her body was tired and beat up from fifty years of smoking and she was dying. Her body was just worn out and it was only a matter of time. This visit was different than most of the others. I was close by her as my siblings lived thousands of miles away. So I had the responsibility of taken care of her. After the usual greeting and the small talk of how are you feeling and what did the doctors say, she asked me a very strange question. Do you have a girlfriend? I was taken aback by this question as I didn't usually bother my Mother with my personal life. She had her own problems and was on a need to know basis. This, she didn't need to know. She persisted like I had never seen before and continued to ask the question. I had no clue where this was coming from as I didn't tell her about Wendy's visit. I finally told her yes "I have a girlfriend" and I tried to figure out now why she was relieved. She wanted to see if I would lie to her. She knew Wendy and liked her a lot as everyone did. But how did she know? My son, who was upset with Wendy stealing a few days of his time, told his Mom, who told her friend whom she knew from the time when she cleaned houses for a living, about the visit.

This friend then told her ex-husband who happened to be my Mothers former boyfriend. The ex-boyfriend was an integral part of fucking up my mother's final days. He extorted money from her ($60.000) during their three year relationship and nobody in my family liked this guy. Actually we couldn't stand him. He was nothing but an obstacle after my Mom got sick and was admitted to the hospital. Well he told my Mom about Wendy's visit. I wondered what this was supposed to accomplish. I think it was his mission to try and destroy me. He wanted control of my mother and what little money she had left that he hadn't somehow pried out of her. I finally connected all he dots and realized that people can be mean and these people need to find better things to do with their lives other than trying to hurt others, especially me. This information and this whole fiasco had accomplished absolutely nothing.

So this raised an interesting question. Were we a couple or not? Wendy and I had to agree on what our status was. We hashed out the pros and cons of the long distant thing and agreed to see each other a minimum of four times a year. I was also planning a vacation to the Cayman Islands for us as a surprise sometime in the next six months. I was squirreling away some money from my part time job for this vacation. We decided to give this long distant relationship a shot. I practically had to drag the words out of her but they finally came. I was really proud to walk around and actually call her my girlfriend.

I was a happy camper! Things went well for weeks but eventually it started to deteriorate as lack of physical contact and great sex was gnawing at us both. We started to drift apart.
I think she wanted to date and I really had no interest in that. Our children were young and it would be four years before everyone was out of high school. We decided to take a break. Should I say she decided to take a break and I agreed? That's better.

Wendy's oldest daughter who was living at home started to make a joke about her Mom's trip calling it "Humpty Dumpty". Neither Wendy nor I knew what it meant so we had to get clarification from an 11 year old. It is when some sleeps with someone they are seeing, knowing full well that they are dumping them afterwards. We both thought it was funny in the beginning, but now that we are "taking a break" it's not funny anymore. My son and I were still not speaking as this went on for six weeks. He was still mad about that visitation night and the whole three day thing. I think his real frustration was that I was seeing someone or anyone other than his mother. He referred to her as "my little whore from up north". There was no visitation during the next six weeks, just a few emails from me letting him know, that when he was ready to see me, to let me know. I didn't understand completely because his Mom was on her second boyfriend since we separated. I didn't understand the double standard.

18

As time went on we stayed in touch. Emails and phone calls became less and less. Wendy became annoyed when I asked for more. I wanted more and I still wanted that **_something special_** back in my life. We started to fight on the phone and sometimes I would go days without hearing from her. So being childish, as we all can be, I played the game and slowed my responses to her emails and sometimes intentionally let her calls go to voice mail.

She began dating and explained that she needed to do that more then I wanted to. She was a sex addict and had to have her needs met on a regular basis. Masturbation wasn't cutting it for her and we were no longer having phone sex. She did explain that she had great orgasms while masturbating and she used to have quickies with herself in the tanning salon.

I figured that what's good for the goose is good for the gander. So I decided to date as well. It was also her recommendation that I also date as it would make her feel more justified about her dating. I didn't really want to because I figure if I waited twenty-seven years the first time; I could wait and was willing to wait a few more years. I shopped around at some prospects and started some innocent dating. There were breakfast dates, coffee at Starbucks and attending local events. There were no real dates like dinner and a movie or a day at the beach. There were just no real quality replacements for Wendy. I became less and less interested in dating other women. Most of my dates didn't go very far. There was some stupid reason I was staying sexually faithful. I was in love with Wendy.

There was one woman that I wanted to date on a regular basis. We started a small business together trying to help internet helpless people sell their unwanted things of value on Craig's List. I also had access to used furniture in my job and developed a good working knowledge of the resale value of used stuff. At one point, this woman basically asked me to steel stuff for her so she could resell it and make a profit. It pissed her off when I told her I would never do that. I think that showed the differences in our character. She said she had just moved and needed some furniture. I asked her what she needed most and she said a dining room set. Her apartment was not very big and she was looking for a small dinette with a drop leaf table. I had a lot of used furniture hanging around my house from my Mom's house. She passed away a few months after Wendy's trip to see me. I sent her some pics of the stuff I had and she chose a butcher block, three piece dinette with a drop leaf table. I figured that I would just give it to her. I hoped maybe this woman would finally sexually satisfy me. I really needed to get my brains fucked out as I was still Jonesing the good Wendy sex. I didn't have much time invested in it, as I love to refinish wood, so I brought it by her house. She thanked me and we continued to peruse this used stuff internet helpless business and we scored our first big deal. We took photos and did the Craig's list thing and the deal was, we would split the *profit* 50/50 and I would get the delivery job. On our first job, we sold most of the client's furniture, she kept all the money and someone else got the delivery job. I was pissed to say the least. I stopped buy her house to collect my money and I noticed that the dinette set was missing. When I inquired about its whereabouts, she told me she sold it. I told her we're done!!

So dating wasn't working out for me so I decided to stay busy, delivering furniture on the side, working my two jobs and just hanging out with my male friends. That was now my life. I still spoke to Wendy but it wasn't the same. We swapped dating stories, which really hurt because I really didn't have any to tell her. I was taking better care of myself lately and I paid some bills and bought some new clothes and stuff for myself with the nine hundred dollars I had saved up for our trip to the Cayman Islands. Opps I forgot to tell her about the trip. It's too late now. Sorry Wendy. I had been to the Caymans before and loved it there. So I knew my way around the three islands and it seemed to be an ideal vacation for us. When I finally told her about it she wanted to go. What. Was she Bipolar? What part didn't she get? You can't have your cake and eat it too. I researched the trip and looked at hotel rooms and airfares. We had taken trips together before meeting somewhere, flying in from different parts of the country. I have a son in college some twelve hundred miles away, so I was pretty good at planning travel arrangements. He would fly home six times a year. She bragged about all her dates, the boys who tried to pick her up while bartending at the water park and all her dates to the casino where she always scored big. I found out much later from Wendy's old friend Karen that she probably led me to believe that she was dating more than she actually was, just to make me jealous. More games we played. I hate games.

19

Bartending is a not only a job, it's an art and a lifestyle. If you have never tended bar than you probably have no idea how difficult and fun it is at the same time. It requires skills, coordination, knowledge and a great personality. First are the skills. You need to be fast, efficient, accurate at not only making the drinks, but performing cash register transactions. This includes ringing up checks, running tabs, credit cards and making change for cash customers. Second is coordination. You need to have great hand-eye coordination as your movements are various, your speed needs to be incredible and you need to be able to move in a way that gets you around all night. If you're working with others, you need to know how to stay out of their way. It's like having great sex with a great partner. This coordination is better known to those of us in the industry as "Doing the Dance". Third is the knowledge of all that liquor. There is the difference between sour mash and bourbon or the difference between a cordial and an aperitif. It also requires the knowledge of all those drinks. That includes all the oldies like Sidecars and Presbyterians and all the new ones like Sex on the Beach, Blow Jobs, and Screaming Orgasms; just to name a few. Last is a great personality. You need to be able to handle stress and have your best money making game face on all the time. Being in the weeds and greeting a guest like you are so happy to see them is an art.

Picking up the bartender is a status dream. Your friends would be jealous if they knew you were going to go out with the hot bartender. You meet so many people and good looking people as well. Everybody loves the bartender. You are in the driver's seat to choose who and if you want to go out with. Opportunity is always present. You can get laid anytime you want.

I know, I was a bartender for years and my favorite job was at a tiki bar on the beautiful Gulf of Mexico. One day during Spring Break, two girls in bikinis were asking me for shot recipes. I made them some York Peppermint Patties followed my some Screaming Orgasms. They chugged and laughed and were having a real good time. Then the best looking girl asked me if I knew what a blow job was. I told her yes, but it's been a while. She said "no silly it's a shot". I said yes and she ordered five of them. The key to drinking a Blow Job is two things. First, you are not allowed to use your hands. You have to pick the shot glass up using only your mouth. Second is you have to swallow the whole thing. I made five shots as she had invited a few friends by now, and served them up. She then asked me if they could do them right off the bar. I said no problem. It was a Sunday night and it was slow. There was only one family there at the other end of the pool. I went inside, as this was a lobby bar/ pool bar and I had to take care of both sides. When I came back out one of the girls was lying across the bar on her back in what resembled a tiny bathing suit and the other girls placed the shot glasses, one between her boobs and one in her crotch. The other girls retrieved the shots from there, using their mouths and slammed down the Blow Jobs. These girls were a lot of fun. They were staying down the street in a condo, but I decided to use the pick and choose rule and decided not to pursue any of them, as they all were too hammered at this point, to be of any use to anybody. I love bartending!

There are some let's say interesting or unique people who hold the title of bartender. First I remember Monica. Monica was an alcoholic and a whore. One day she was late for her day shift which started at ten-thirty in the morning. For us morning people that was late. We usually start sometime after five am. I called her cell and her home phone and got no response. I was concerned. Even with the lifestyle she maintained, her attendance was extremely good. I returned to my office on the seventh floor, the bar was located on the lobby level, to tell the staff I had to call in a replacement for her and I would be downstairs opening the bar. As I approached the back door to the kitchen I saw Monica strutting down the hallway. There were only two things on the seventh floor, the restaurant and the suites. She was leaving a suite, hair all wet and obviously she had spent the night with a guest. What a piece of work.

Next there was Leslie. She was also an alcoholic and a slut. There was a problem with the lobby bar as the restaurant was on the seventh floor so there was limited supervision on the lobby level. No one really ever knew when I was there, especially during my divorce. I spent more time there than I wanted to. It was better than the alternative of going home and engaging in fights with the wife over insignificant things. I would pop into the bar on occasion, sometimes late at night and witness her drinking shots with customers and engaged in the pick-up process. As a bartender, you are supposed to pretend to pick up customers to increase your tips. You are not exactly supposed to pick them up and take them home. Doing shots with them is definitely against corporate policy!

Lastly there was Michelle. She was more of a thief than anything else. I would walk in on a full bar and then would be no checks open. How is that possible? All her friends were there and drinking for free. I had a disciplinary talk with her and she looked at me like I had three heads. So her solution was to charge each of her friends for the first drink and the rest were on the house. So anytime I walked into the bar it LOOKED LIKE everyone was paying. One problem, it was my bar not hers. She got fired just like Monica and Leslie did. Most like I said most; bartenders are thieves, alcoholics and whores. Remember I used to be a bartender. You can make a good living bartending on the up and up, you don't have to steal.

20

So the dating game continued, as I listened to Wendy tell me how this guy asked her out from the bar and this one from the hospital. She filled me in on all her dates and sometimes in detail like the guy she met at the gym. They went out, dinner, movie, she met his daughter, yada yada yada! This was killing me as I was not really ever dating anyone. I was always waiting for her to get over her need to date and settle down with me.

I decided to quit drinking beer a short while after Wendy went home. She didn't like my drinking, but she knew better not to push her AA crap on me. I just went to the store one day to buy beer and I just said NO! After I quit she always tried to get me to go to meetings. No thanks. I didn't need help last time and I don't need help this time. I quit for two years. There were no sponsors and no meetings. I will tell when I started drinking again later. We stayed in touch by email mostly. The jokes continued to fly and I used to write songs and poetry, so I would send her some of my arranged thoughts from time to time. Here is an example:

07-01-09
Wendy

Remember that night in Kansas
City, my last night in town
I asked you to move to New
Jersey, I thought you'd say no,
but you didn't

After we broke up and I was
heartbroken and you moved out
I thought you hated me and
would vow never to see me
again, but you didn't

Two and a half decades has past
and you're back in my life, I thought
after all this time,
you would figure out you
wouldn't want to be with a loser
like me, but you didn't

Things were going great, emails
and two hour phone calls, I
thought we would plan
your trip here together and you
would consult me, but you didn't

So you arrived in great style
and fashion and we hit it off, I
thought we wouldn't get along
as well or you would do
something to make me
uncomfortable, but you didn't

A perfectly grown woman, I couldn't
get enough of you, I loved you
even more,
broke and depressed I thought
you would complain, but you
didn't

Trouble with my son and the
email thing, the trust and lost
confidence
I figured you would dump me for
good, but you didn't

Summer came, you got busy I
understand , emails got shorter,
the phone calls got less

I got excited you were
supposed to visit in August, but
you didn't

You built me up and brought my
self esteem to a new level,
you've been through so much, I
respected that in you, I figured
you would give up on me, but
you didn't

Love trust and honesty, no
matter what the cost, made us
what we were
I thought I was getting brushed
off and that you lied to me, but
you didn't

I think of you always and
dreamed of our lives together
forever and ever
I figured we could seal the deal
when you came to visit me after the
summer was over, but you didn't

———————

I received a text message one night
that she was in the hospital. She

was not working, she was admitted. She was highly allergic to bees and had been stung by a swarm outside her apartment. I became immediately concerned as if you had ever witnessed someone in that condition, it's not pretty. I was glad she was in the hospital and being cared for. She had the attending physician, takes some pics with her phone and sent them to me. We texted for hours as if you have ever been in any Emergency Room you know that four hours is an average stay and it is usually a very boring four hours. There was no TV and no one to talk to so texting me was a good idea. Her face was all swollen, no make-up and just a mess. I stilled loved her but had to make a little joke about her appearance (which I don't even recall), which she didn't appreciate. I can be an asshole sometimes. Of course when you are sick you're not really in the mood for anything except meds and sleep. We all just want to get better. After three hours of texting back and forth Wendy is thinking that she is about to get checked out and go home. She made some calls and was getting a ride home, as the doctor would not let her drive while on this medication. I asked who was driving her home and she did not answer but became upset with my question. I asked the question again and she not only became furious with me but she told me it was her ex-husband and that she would call me tomorrow. The doctor told her to take the next day off. I replied with an "Okay" and went to bed.

Wendy was Bipolar. She was taking medication for it but sometimes I don't know if it was working as well as I wished it was. During this "long distance relationship", she became short tempered with me several times and she made us cool off on more than a few occasions. Bipolar people run hot and cold and it's like they are two different people. It is a mood disorder. Her mood swings were extreme and I always had trouble handling them but I knew she was bipolar and taking medication for it. Most of the time she was on an extreme high, life is great type of moods. Sometimes she would just tell me forget it, we're done, it's over, don't talk to me anymore and I just swallowed it because I knew she really loved me. The only part I really disliked was the Game. The one we played after a spat and the unspoken wait as to who was going to break down and call or email first. When I would break down first, I would get "what took you so long? When she would break down and make the first move, it was like it never happened, Bipolar!

She didn't call the next day and I couldn't stop worrying and wondering how she was. If you recall, giving Wendy medication can be dangerous as she is an addictive person. I waited until my lunch hour and called my baby to see how she was. Well good old Bipolar kicked in and she gave me an ass chewing on the phone. She said she was shopping with her daughter and everything was fine. She was almost upset and rude to me on the phone. We hung up but I was determined to email her later as now I was concerned, as the phone calls made from her to me became almost nonexistent. I sent the email that I spent hours creating to make sure I got it right. She replied with the message that she had her life and I had mine (both of which consisted of a bunch of fabricated exaggerations) and we were ultimately done. Wow!

At this point I'm not sure I should have quit drinking as my soul mate just told me to fuck-off! Let me guess, this is probably another game. How fun. I wonder how long we wait this time and who will break first. I waited the normal corporate cooling off period of three days and then surged forward. This was getting ridiculous. First we are together and then we are not. I fired off an email explaining my frustrations and told her how much I loved her. She replied back with the long distance thing is not working as she needs to date to survive and that we are breaking up. She suggested we should be friends and not loose what we have regained like last time. She said you can never have too many friends. I agreed and decided that having her as a friend was better than not having her at all. I figured that someday she'd be ready to settle down with her only real option, me.

21

Emails continued but became less and less frequent. I would drop her casual notes from time to time. She still emailed me with details of her dating life which only hurt to read but I began to become numb. She continued to tell me about her exciting life (mine was not), including family stuff and work so I listened and responded in a friendly manner. Here is an example as to what I would send her.

"I just thought I would drop you a line to say Hello. I'm sure you're busy with summer and are looking forward to a restful cruise in November. I hope you daughter enjoyed her trip to Grandmas and your son did well in the Little League World Series. All is great here no need to worry."

She continued to meet and date men and give me feedback, now which happened probably every week or two. Apparently, unlike me and most of the men she has dated (slept with) in the past were not as well endowed as this new Beau. I would like to believe that size doesn't matter. I am afraid to admit it does. Wendy became infatuated with this twenty-four year old man that was carrying a twelve-incher. I dated a girl once (Jodi) who told me of the sexual pleasures of a large penis and I was not one to argue as I was not in that category. She said that not only was it the size during penetration, it was the ability to utilize more positions during sex. She said she thought of staying with this guy only for the "Big Dick Syndrome". I guess size really does matter. I was not about to take penis enlargement pills just to compete as that is not what I am about. Wendy was the one with the fake boobs. There would be nothing artificially enhanced about me. I knew two women with large breasts in the past. One I dated when I was sixteen years old and they were amazingly soft and completely real. Back then boob jobs were relatively non-existent except for the very wealthy. The other woman I slept with once was a woman named

Marybeth, nicknamed Marybreast.They were very large, maybe a D-cup and very real. I think I only slept with her as an achievement due to the size of her breast. It was a one night stand and we both knew that. I just loved playing with those puppies.

She continued to torment me with the details of this relationship. She was concerned a little herself because this man not only had sex with her, as a man so well endowed could have and probably was having sex with a lot of women much younger. At this point Wendy was almost fifty years old. I am pretty sure she understood this but didn't want to admit it. She became annoyed with me again (Bipolar) and refused to discuss it with me further. So we were on the complete outs again and I backed off even more and had contact with her in short emails every two or three weeks. Then out of the blue she sent me an email with only an attachment. I opened the attachment and it was a Pic of the boyfriend's big slong, no message. I thought that was just rude. She once explained that I didn't understand what is was like when you meet someone who just satisfies your sexual needs beyond your wildest dreams. Really! I was punishing myself too much and I didn't need it. I was on the upswing and I had gained ten of the fifteen pounds I promised her and was starting to look pretty good. My self esteem was high and I did want a deterrent. I loved Wendy to death but I was not going to sink into another hole because of her inconsiderate behavior.

Life is pretty boring at this juncture in my life. I am not dating. I think I know enough about women and life that I really don't need to be bothered with the aggravation of dating that accompanies the process. It's also expensive which I consider a waste of time and money. I stay positive waiting for a life changing event. Lord knows I need one right now. I am still working out and still not drinking now over two years sober. Wendy didn't think I could do it without help, so nana nana booboo! My youngest son is away at college outside

Detroit, some twelve hundred miles away, so my house is empty now. I am suffering from another illness now called "Empty Nest Syndrome". Let's just say life is fairly quiet for me now and I am okay with that. I really don't have any choice. I sign up for some dating services, you know you can look at your matches for free. I thought I could handle some window shopping right now. That's really all I was interested in. It is a strange thing that when we are younger, we are attracted to looks. As we become more experienced and older we are attracted to a certain look. Lauren Bacall explains it best in her book "By Myself". It's a certain look that you notice in a person that tells you this could be the one. It's what Bogie saw in Bacall and what I saw in Wendy that I would look for again, a look. I didn't see much point in my life or much movement in any direction. Working out had no purpose except for myself, which was still a pretty good reason and my career, well, I didn't really have one. I applied for jobs constantly, but no one wants to hire an over the hill manager with more experience than they do. No comfort or longevity in that. So I am waiting tables and spending my nights working out, reading, watching TV and spending time with my two best friends, my dogs. Let me tell you something, without them I probably wouldn't have made it. They are truly man's best friend as they always greet you like they haven't seen you in a while and they listen implicitly. They never talk back and they can always tell when you are hurting, inside or out.

So then one day it happens. An older waitress, mid forties, blonde, attractive, suggests we go out for a beer after work. Then she catches herself and says, "I'm sorry, I forgot you don't drink". I thought for a quick minute and said "screw it, let's go get that beer". We went to a local pub and had a few (can never have just one). It's like eating a Lay's potato chip. I had a really good time. I never had more than three which is my legal limit as I will never go through the pain and expense of a DUI again. _That's when I starting drinking again._ It became my social life even if it was only an hour a day maybe two to three times a week.

Sometime later after trying to forget about the only woman I ever wanted to be with, I would receive a message from Wendy that would turn out to be yet, another final straw. Wendy sent me an email one day and said that her Dad, who lived a few miles from me, was in need of a medical procedure and she would be flying down for the week to be with him. Her Dad maybe lived 15 miles away and we both looked at this as an opportunity to get together. We were not as close as we were during her visit and all that we expected from each other was a meal together. I told her I could make myself free any time. I worked weekends which gave me a day off during the week and most of my nights were free. I only worked two nights a week at the restaurant. She agreed and forwarded me her itinerary. She was staying for a week and I was just down the road so it looked pretty good that we would get together. She asked if I would mind getting together with her Mom or Dad or both during her visit. I told her it didn't matter to me. I was flexible. I was still thinking that my soul mate and I were going to be together forever so I guess it time to meet the parents. I met her Mom once before, but it was a long time ago and it was only for five minutes in New Jersey, so I really don't recall.

We struggled to get together as we emailed back and forth several times daily. She always had a conflict. I could make adjustments to make it happen. She was not being flexible. The week started to erode as time passed and it was nearing her departure date. I became desperate. I always knew that everytime I saw Wendy, I had an effect on her that put her back in total love with me. I needed to see her. A one hour meal could have done this, but at this point it didn't look like it was going to happen. I was becoming desperate as the week was almost over and I made one last effort. I told her I would drive to her departing airport (an hour away) to have dinner in her hotel the night before she flew home. Bipolar was back as she became furious. I thought that it was a pretty generous offer. I didn't ask to spend the night (as I had to go to work the next day at six in the morning); I just wanted to see her. She fussed in her email and it was too late to respond so I called her. She freaked out on me claiming that all men were the same and all I wanted to do was sleep with her. I didn't have to sleep with her to get high. Just being with her in that comfort zone was better than any sex I have ever had. She cancelled dinner and said she was flying home in the morning but no thank you to dinner. I'll tell you, with the shit I put up with from her I probably should have dumped her or not gotten back together with her after twenty-seven years. I am trying to rebuild my life and she is just tearing me down. I have had enough already. I told her to have a great flight and I would talk to her later. She abruptly said good-bye and hung up the phone. Hum?

At this point I am pretty certain this is finally and completely over. I am distraught as I really thought that I would spend the rest of my life (whatever time there was) with her.

That feeling of being with her and that **something special**, I never wanted to end. I sent her one last email.

Wendy,
I thought you were a bigger person than
doing this via telephone instead of doing it in person. After all we have been through so much.
You can't keep messing with my heart like
this. It causes me pain, lack of sleep
and unhappiness. It's not fair to me. I am sorry this whole thing ever happened
because in the end I got hurt,
AGAIN
and I'm a little tired of you hurting me.
I guess this time it is really over. Don't do me any favors
like
emails or an occasional phone call, it
just hurts too much. CUT THE CORD!
Don't call me when you're ready, because
I won't be. It was fun while it

lasted and again I thank you for
everything you did for me and it
was
a great deal, even more than you
can imagine. Take care and good
luck.
Someday
I hope you get everything you
want.
John

So that was it, it was finally over and I could move on with my life although I would never forget her. "It starts in my toes and crinkles my nose", you know. But boy what a run and what a story. I often wondered what would happen if we did get back together. I could be the happiest man in the world. I spent my life observing couples. I have made some interesting observations over the years. The key to a successful relationship is two words, "Yes Dear". I was good at saying that to her. I noticed couples who fought all the time and I noticed the special couples who never had to speak, never argued and were just totally in love as I wished Wendy and I were. Over all the long years we knew each other, I picture myself living with her in Florida, kids are in college and we are just together, that's all that would matter. Oh well. I guess not. I wasn't playing the game anymore. I wasn't going to torture myself anymore. I never wrote her or emailed her again.

Time goes on and though I will never forget her, although I will try to. For anyone to possess that *something special* that makes anyone feels the way she made me feel is priceless. It's probably something most people never find and unfortunately will never experience. You can't get closer to heaven that that feeling. At this point in my life I have been burned by her and my three ex-wives and have no interest in trying to date anyone. I will be happy with my drinking buddy a few hours a week. There is nothing going on between her and me as we are just co-workers and friends and there is no real attraction to each other sexually. Don't get me wrong she is very attractive, but there is a compatibility factor that we were missing. She was Blonde, tanned, had large real breasts and was kind of sexy in her own way. She was about forty and in good shape, but no, I guess by now I should be able to recognize that the chemistry would never be there. Now if we became friends with benefits, which would be okay with me, but that never happened as a short time later she fell in love with her new boss after she stopped working with me. There is another mistake about to happen for her. You don't dip you pen in the company inkwell!

From time to time Wendy crossed my mind and I had mixed emotions. I loved her and hated her at the same time. I always hated playing the game and I guess I figured that in a few years after she figured out that no one loved her like I did or ever would and that size doesn't matter in the long term scheme of things that she would come back to me. But I was not going to break down and go after her.
I would remain stubborn and not give in, ever!
I was kind of tired of getting dumped although

I always remained hopeful. I was a hopeless romantic.

They say that a in a healthy relationship you should never go to bed mad at each other. It's probably true. We however stayed mad at each other for over two years. I often thought about burying the hatchet and being the bigger person, and pick up the phone or shoot her an email. I decided against it all the time. I was just going to wait and if she never ever called or emailed me again. I would, in my heart, wish her the best, would hope that she would finally find happiness. Of course I didn't ever believe she would find the happiness that she found with me. Oh well, time just continued to crawl forward. Two of my favorite quotes that are my creed and the way I live my life are as follows;

"I shall pass this way but
once, any good therefore,
that I can do or any kindness
that
I can show to any human being.
 Let
me do it now. Let me not defer
nor
neglect it, for I shall not pass
this way again."
Stephen Grellet

And

"God grant me the serenity
to accept the things I cannot
change;
courage to change the things I
can;
and wisdom to know the
difference.

Living one day at a time;
Enjoying one moment at a time;
Accepting hardships as the

pathway to peace;
Taking, as He did, this sinful
world
as it is, not as I would have it;
Trusting that He will make all
things right
if I surrender to His Will;
That I may be reasonably happy
in this life
and supremely happy with Him
Forever in the next.
Amen."

Reinhold Niebuhr

22

I never heard from Wendy except once again and I thought about her constantly. There was a coffee cup with her name on it at work, as we bought used coffee cups from second hand stores. Most of them had names on them. That one always made me think about her. I thought about her less and less as I couldn't punish myself any longer. My life continued on as work kept me busy and my friends filled the gap of companionship. I kept delivering furniture on my off time, kept working at the restaurant and was promoted to store manager at the new retail store that my non-profit opened a short time later. Life was okay and I was okay. My son and I patched things up although not much was ever said again. At least we were talking and getting along pretty good. The divorce dust had settled and his Mom and I actually became friends again. We would attend his theatrical performances together and would actually travel together in the same car. I had no complaints. I wasn't dating as I really wasn't into it or trying to find someone who could replace Wendy. I just went without. It was a hassle dating anyway and it was still something I considered a waste of money. I figured it was a win-win situation, save money and no bullshit. My son, now in college, occupied most of my efforts as it was expensive and it was long distance. Traveling home for holidays was the biggest expense and trying to support him and continue the relationship I wanted to have with him was now my priority. Life was good and I started writing a Blog about servers in the hospitality business. It started to catch on. People thought it was entertaining and funny. I received several comments about how people liked my writing. It was a cool site connected to Facebook and Twitter and I was happy with the results. As Wendy would say all the time "Life is Good'. I watched the movie "The Shinning" the other night and forgot that the wife in the movie's name was Wendy. The part Jack Nicolson played was Johnny. So the scene where he is chopping down the door and says "Wendy, Johnny's Home" produced a memory flash back for me. Some people used to call me Johnny.

Most of what I remember about Wendy is her huge heart. She was a very caring person, from being with me and through both my parents' deaths, she was great. As you recall she attended my Dad's funeral and I lost my mother a short time after Wendy and I broke up for the last time. There actually was an email I sent her when I told Wendy that my Mother had passed. She actually responded with a phone call. It was nice that she called to offer her sincere condolences. Other than that it was a very short conversation. My mind was obviously somewhere else. Once again Wendy showed that **something special** and that big heart of hers. We never spoke again!

Quite some time has passed now and life has changed for me a little as I am no longer working for the retail store as a manager. Not only is the tiny salary gone which is insignificant in the scheme of things, but now the benefit package is gone and the extra money making furniture deliveries after work is gone as well. My income has taken a severe nose dive as I am only working at the restaurant full time now. The money I make there was actually more than I made working as a store manager. The deliveries were just a pure bonus. There were no medical benefits which became rather expensive. The fifty-five dollar prescription became over two hundred dollars as well as all the other shit the doctors had me taking. I soon realized that all the medications they had me taking were unnecessary. I quit smoking so that eliminated most of the medications. I could write another book about what I think is wrong with the medical system in this country and maybe I will, but not right now. As Tom Hanks said in "Sleepless in Seattle" when asked how he survived after his wife's death, he said "you just get up everyday and breathe in and out". So that is where I was right now. A couple of more years had passed and I was still waiting and hoping inside that she would break the ice and call or email. I looked for emails for a while but stopped after a few months and gave up looking. Maintaining my stubbornness, I would not give in. How could she possibly live without me? I was a good catch back then and I am still am now. I'm still good looking, and taking good care of myself. I love to cook, as I cook for one all the time except when I can catch my college age son home. I am a handyman around the house, mechanically inclined and great in bed. What more could any woman ask for?

We had a conversation in the restaurant one day about what ever happened to your high school sweetheart. We talked about the benefits of Facebook and the internet. I explained I had found some old friends, classmates and girlfriends on Facebook and that the internet was a great tool to find old flames. I decided to look up my high school sweetheart when I got home. I was successful yet disappointed as to what I found. She was successful but had let herself go. She was probably sixty pounds overweight. I am funny that way. At one point in my life I was overweight, drank like a fish, had a heart attack, but I fixed it all. It hurt a lot but I did it. It's all about the person inside you and what YOU want to do with your life. Yeah, it hurts but if you want anything bad enough, you'll go after it. Wendy also looked great her entire life. She had her struggles with life and she also beat them. So I am sorry, I do not have much respect for people who don't care enough about themselves to look their best. While on the internet, I did some more research and decided to go to my Facebook account. Searching for friends I noticed a friend suggestion for Wendy. I thought this was strange, but it was an email host driven response as I was trying to improve my audience for my Blog. She had a Facebook account so I couldn't help myself. I starting digging. It was odd because there appeared to never be any activity. She had some people listed under friends and they were all family. There was her Mom, her Dad, and her oldest son who attended college in Florida. I thought this to be strange so I dug a little deeper. I went to the World Wide Web, which is where she found out all the information about me, which generated the letter she sent me after twenty-seven years. I went to the World Wide Web and typed in her full name and the first thing that popped up was an obituary for a woman with the same name. I clicked on the link and my heart stopped. It was Wendy. Something inside me just died.

23

I read further and she had passed away over a year and a half ago. I am sick with guilt and confused as she was the healthiest woman I knew and so young. I read the entire obituary and was still in disbelief. There were also photos of her and her family and this confirmed that it was her. She was only fifty years old.

I got up from my computer and walked around my house several times in total disbelief. So many things were going through my mind. There was my love for her, my frustrations with her and the dream I had of her with our lives together someday. There was a lot of guilt. Why didn't I call her after six months or so? Why didn't she call me or drop me one of those lengthy emails? Questions, questions and more questions! I had no one I could call. I was completely lost. I know I was going to hear "don't beat yourself up" when my friends and family found out. I never told my son about her death as he never liked the woman anyway, a woman he had never met. That was just not fair to her. She would have been God's best choice for a Step-Mom for him. That's one of the great things about living alone, you can beat yourself up all you want and no one can stop you. I didn't cry at first as the shock kept me at bay. I didn't know what to do. I poured a good glass of Pinot Noir and sipped it and pondered. A lot of "what if" questions went through my mind. Saddened by the discovery of this news and now a little relaxed after the wine I went to bed. It was quite late. Tomorrow, I told myself, I need to find out what had happened.

Feeling nothing the next morning except remorse, still beating myself up, I could not hide my demeanor at work. Some people who were close to me asked what's up. I explained the short version as none of my co-workers had ever met her, when she was here. They were not employed back then. They expressed their condolences. I rushed straight home as discovery was on my agenda with a determination that nobody was going to stop. I fried up the old PC and started searching. I started with the obituary and read it over and over again. I was looking for clues as to a cause of death. I found nothing other than donations can be made to the American Heart Association and the American Red Cross. I thought to myself Heart Attack? This could not be possible as she was all cleaned up from drug use and abuse, didn't drink, didn't smoke, and lived a good life, even if it was without me (little sarcasm). I came up empty. Next I tried a local internet search in and around her home town. I looked for newspaper articles for accidents and tragedies. I found nothing. I searched for hours and found zip!

I am now confused but have no contact information for her family. I remembered that her son had a Facebook page. I struggled to find it and finally did. I sent him the following message.

*Hi ******. My name is **** ********** and I knew your mother for a very long time, 30+ years. I just heard* *the news (1 year+ late) and want to say how sorry I am for your loss. I was just curious as to what happened? The last time I saw her was three years ago. We lost touch. Please let me know. Sorry to bring back any pain and again my condolences.*

I waited days and didn't persist but the waiting was killing me inside. I never did get a reply. I am a persistent person, ask anybody, so I wasn't giving up.

So I needed some therapy and decided to prescribe myself some treatment. I retrieved some photographs of her from her last visit with me and stared at them for a few hours. I then selected one and used it as my desktop background. I needed to look at her every day!

My next treatment was to express myself in words as I always like to write, Duh! I mentioned I wrote a Blog. The Blog was for all to see but it was based on Hospitality Servers and Bartenders and it commented on all the fun we have and all the crazy zany shit that happens in our business. It's called Serving for a Living. Com. Depending on when you are reading this book it may still be active and enjoyed by many. Most people think it's funny and an accurate depiction of what really happens in our field. It is connected to a Facebook page and a Twitter page with the same name. Right now, since my mind is much clouded, I cannot write any Blogs. I actually can't do much of anything right now. I just found out my soul mate is gone. So I wrote a Blog about Wendy and posted it on the site. It went as follows;

Fallen Friends

TODAY;
I learned today that a loved one passed away. It happened over a year ago. We were in love over thirty years ago and reunited three years ago. We dreamed, remembered, loved and laughed and promised to see each other again. It was an amazing weekend. It was unfortunate that the last time we spoke we were upset with each other and in our

stubbornness, told ourselves that we would never speak again. I knew this would pass as we both had our families and busy lives in different parts of the country, but we were always friends. I just figured we would make amends sooner or later and take that trip to the Cayman Islands that I always promised her. I guess I let too much time pass, as in a recent internet search, trying to see what she had been up to, I ran across her obituary.

She was only 50. Losing people affects you, as I was useless at work today. It gets buried inside you and becomes this big deep hole of ache. It doesn't magically go away after you officially stop mourning. If you have ever lost a loved one, then you know exactly how it feels, and if you have not, you cannot possibly imagine how I feel.

TOMORROW;
This really has nothing to do with serving for a living, but it is all that is on my mind. I will go on

***and the pain will go away. The
great memories will live on
forever. In the future I will learn to
rectify my differences sooner
rather than later. You should too.
If tears could build a stairway and
memories build a lane, I'd walk
right up to heaven and bring you
home again. I will always love
you Wendy!!!!***

I few Blog followers came in the
next day and offered their
condolences and I thought that was
helpful and I appreciated it
immensely. But I still didn't know
what happened and I wasn't giving
up. I was torn between some lines
of ethics right now. If I find her
parents, do I want to drudge this up
again just for my satisfaction? I tried
to look up her parents up on
facebook anyway and struck out.
They were in their seventies and
most likely didn't have a Facebook
page, although they were listed on
her Facebook page. I tried a local
white pages search for their last
known location that I had for the

both of them and came up empty. I am by no means languid so I would continue to persist.

I decide my next treatment would be to work out. Strange you say, but no, it helps me think. Adrenaline is an amazing force. As I went through my routine, I remembered that this was something Wendy got me doing religiously again after her visit. The results were impressive this time. The reps were higher in count and the weights I lifted were greater and I don't know if I was mad or motivated. It doesn't matter because it was a very good workout, no matter how you look at it. It cleared my head. I got an idea. I remember seeing a "contact me" link on the internet obituary, so I returned to the site. I reread every word until I discovered a message to Wendy from a friend stating that they were best friends since middle school and how much she would miss her, etc., etc... I clicked on the link which provided me with an email address. This was the lifelong friend I spoke about. My message was as follows;

I knew Wendy for many years. I don't know if you remember, but I took Wendy to New Jersey a long time ago and just learned of her passing. I really need to know what happened. Please reply.

Days had passed and there was no response. I am now looking at her pictures on my computer, the pictures we took when she was here. It finally hit me that she is gone. I am now in tears and in deep sorrow as I now realize I will never see her again. I am reliving the weekend that she was here in every detail. I think the heart helps the brain remember the important stuff.

More days have passed and I am starting to think I will never know what happened to the love of my life. I told myself, I am not going to let her go until I find out what happened. I figured my next step was to contact the coroner's office for an autopsy report. I know that's pretty extreme but I am bothered by this so much I will not rest until I find out what happened. Day in and day out I ponder and I get no satisfaction from not knowing. I get home from work about a week after I sent her best friend the email and there is a response in my in-box. It reads as follows:

Just realized I could get Ur email address from Ur entry. Didn't see it on the cell screen for a bit? Oh well, yep, heartbroken doesn't even begin to explain the loss of Wendy's passing. Do feel free to call my cell that would prob be more comfortable in this situation. If u don't think so, then obviously, just email or text me back w/ Ur concerns.

I really hate when people use text language in an email. That's not important. She apparently posted a comment to me on a website she maintains in Wendy's honor, messaging me to contact her. I had not returned to the obituary site in a week or so as it was too painful. I paced for a short time and cleared my calendar of all events and made the call. I started to introduce myself and she stopped me. She said my name is Karen and I know all about you and have since the beginning. She was the friend that Wendy confided in all this time since our beginning. She knew everything about our relationship, going back thirty years, and the reunion. It was eerie. I felt as if I knew this woman. She definitely knew who I was. It was almost like talking to Wendy. She was familiar with way too much information! I was uncomfortable at first. After talking to her for a while, she became an instant ally. She knew all the details of the reunion as well as all the "fighting" and "breaking up" and she even knew details about my son reading our emails. I think she might have been the one to convince her to forget about the email breach and move on. I made some reference to Wendy' dating life and the problems that it caused during our long distance relationship and she told me that Wendy didn't date as much as she may have led me to believe. It was just another version of the game. She played that game with me about her life and later it proved not to be a fun game in the end. I felt after talking with her for a short while that I owed her a debt of gratitude. Maybe she helped keep us together all these years. I don't know and never will.

She inquired as to how I found out about her death. It happened a year and a half prior, so some time had passed. I explained how I discovered the bad news and how I contacted her. She went on to explain the details. Karen lived about an hour away so they didn't see each other much but kept in constant communication, emails, telephone, etc...
She said Wendy was supposed to be going somewhere on her days off, I don't remember where, but she couldn't contact her. She called and left voice messages and text messages but there was no reply. When you are that close to someone, you don't ignore their phone calls or text messages. She tried and tried but there was no response. Finally she decided to call her at work on the night she was supposed to return to work. It had been two days. Karen called the hospital and they told her Wendy had not shown up for work nor did she call in. Now extremely worried, as Wendy, like me never missed a

day of work, she got in her car and drove the one hour drive to Wendy's house. She didn't have the ex-husband's phone number and the kids were too young to have cell phones. She arrived at her apartment and there was no answer from knocking on the door. She called the police. That's when they found Wendy, in bed, lifeless and gone.

The coroner was called to remove the body and an autopsy was performed, revealing a high content of Insulin in her bloodstream. The big question was how it got there. Karen told me that there were two possibilities. The first one was that Wendy committed suicide. This is the one most of us didn't believe or want to believe. This was Miss "Life is Good", we're talking about. Wendy's glass was always half full, not half empty. Her life was good and she always talked to Karen about her plans for the future as well as the future of her children. I wasn't going to believe this. I then asked Karen what scenario number two was and horrifying as it was she told me. Wendy's ex-husband murdered her.

We all knew that Wendy was a nurse and giving herself an injection was no big deal. What you don't know is that her ex-husband also had experience with needles as he was and had been a drug addict for years. Karen told me it would not have been hard for him to access the apartment (he had a key because of the shared custody of the kids) and perform this terrible deed, robbing me and the world of Wendy's presence. The coroner listed the cause of death as a suicide. That was unacceptable to everyone. The family then created a cover story for everyone, especially the family and mostly for her children. Wendy died from a heart attack. When I asked Karen why an investigation was never done she told me. It wouldn't bring her back and if her ex-husband was guilty of murder, the kids would have no parent now. So it was left alone. That is why I couldn't find any information on-line about her death. Apparent suicides are not newsworthy stories. Karen told me that her and her ex-husband fought constantly. She said she witnessed an argument in a parking lot once when the kids were switching parents for the week and witnessed one of the most hostile fights she had ever seen. There was verbal mayhem in the parking lot. The part that really bothered Karen was that the kids seemed unaffected by this argument. It seemed to her that they were used to this fighting and it didn't really seem to faze them. Wendy told me that her and her ex-husband got along great. Remember they were friends. He picked her up from the hospital after the bee sting incident and did other favors for her. Apparently Wendy led me to believe some things that were not true. She was painting a prettier picture of her life than what actually was. She always tried to stay positive.

Karen and I continued to talk for what seemed like an hour. She told me that Wendy had touched so many people that there were almost 600 people at her funeral. We both knew she had a huge heart and was a great person. We all agreed she would be greatly missed by all. After reading the entries on her obituary site it was heartbreaking to hear the words that everyone used to describe Wendy. There were terms like her vibrant smile, her bright character, she was intelligent, dazzling, smart, a great listener, a firecracker, a hummingbird, had an amazing spark, dynamic, always had big smiles, gave warm hugs, and was very caring person and a good mother. Regardless, I would never feel that **something special** ever again and I was forever heartbroken.

24

Karen and I spoke for a while longer until the real heartbreaking information came out. She began telling me some of Wendy's feelings about me and some of the details Wendy never told me and probably never would have, even if she continued to live on. I explained to Karen how I felt during the reunion we had and the unbelievable feeling of comfort during her visit. She told me that Wendy had told her *exactly* the same thing. I am still in shock at the explanation of her death and I am in deep sorrow. We continued to talk until she told me of Wendy's plan. Karen said her plan was to wait until both of her children were out of high school, two more years and then she wanted to move to Florida. She said she really didn't like living in the Midwest. Both of Wendy's parents lived here and she learned to love the Gulf Coast of Florida especially after her visit with me. Most importantly she wanted to get back together me and as Karen put it, give it one last try. She told me that Wendy said that she thought I was **THE ONE**!

Some clues started to appear as the question she asked during her visit "how many times per week, do you think we would have sex?" It was Wendy's way of indicating she thought we would be together forever.

I don't know if you believe in soul mates, but I do now. I am now trying to digest all this information as my emotions are now quite mixed. I feel very bad that I didn't make any effort to release my stubbornness and pick up the phone and call her. I never emailed her again. I asked myself the question "could I have helped or changed the outcome of this terrible tragedy in my life"? I will never know! Karen and I ended our conversation and she told me that if I ever wanted to talk or needed some consolation, to call her. I didn't see any reason to contact her again as I felt it would be too painful.

There was no heart attack and there was no bruising on Wendy's body or any other evidence of foul play. Wendy had decided to leave us on her own terms. She would no longer listen to or be influenced by anyone every again. I just still find it strange that she thought she had no other options. But now, she may finally rest in peace.

So now I have my closure and I can let her go. It will be difficult as there are constant reminders of her everywhere. There is the restaurant that I work in where Wendy and I had breakfast. There is the restaurant where we had dinner, not too far from my house. It is also my brother's favorite restaurant. When he comes to visit and we go there to eat, the memories, fond memories, come back to life. There is that damn coffee cup at work. I can't drive by a Wendy's Restaurant without thinking about her. I see her in a lot of the people I meet. I work in a restaurant with a very high volume, and see a lot of people every week.

I spoke to someone in customer service the other day trying to rectify a personal problem. I have learned to get people's names when I call, for a point of reference when and if I have to call back. The agent answered the phone with a salutation and the company name but did not give her name. When I asked her what her name was, of course you guessed it. It was Wendy. I think about her everyday and look at her picture on my desktop as some kind of therapy or torture; I am not sure which it is. I am okay though as I still work out, take care of myself and don't prefer to date, all positive things trust me.

I called my brother (my best friend) as well as sent him an email, informing him of my sad news. I attached a picture of Wendy.

Dave;
I'm sure you remember her as we went together in 1980, 1981, and 1982. She came to visit 3 years ago. I learned today she passed away over 1-1/2 years ago. She was 50 years old. I really loved her and this really sucks. Just an FYI.

He remembered her from the parties at the beach house and the many holidays we spent together as family. He remembered the time she spent with my oldest son and that she spent the weekend with me after we broke up to attend my father's funeral. We spoke on the phone for a while as we do on a regular basis. He replied,

Sorry to hear. I do remember her and she was special.

In a later conversation with him, he explained that everyone has a double. I don't know about that one. I am just starting believing in the soul mate theory. It may take some time to believe in that one. I will not look for a double or a replacement for Wendy as there will not be one. When I looked in her eyes when she was here I could see happiness. I have since looked into other people's eyes and believe I can recognize happiness. Will I ever find happiness again?
Please learn one thing from this book. Games are played in life all the time. If you are mad at someone and become as stubborn as I was,

not to give in and try to rectify the situation, make the call, send that email or write a letter. Clear the air. Rectify your differences sooner rather than later. As we know life can be short and you never know when it's going to be too late to fix, like it is for me.

If tears could build a stairway and memories build a lane, I'd walk right up to heaven and bring you home again. I will always love you Wendy!!!!

The End